Managerial
Communication

Managerial Communication

Evaluating the Right Dose

J. David Johnson
University of Kentucky

Managerial Communication: Evaluating the Right Dose
Copyright © Business Expert Press, 2012.

First published in 2012 by
Business Expert Press, LLC
222 East 46th Street, New York, NY 10017
www.businessexpertpress.com

ISBN-13: 978-1-60649-464-6 (paperback)

ISBN-13: 978-1-60649-465-3 (e-book)

DOI 10.4128/9781606494653

Business Expert Press Corporate Communication collection

Collection ISSN: 2156-8162 (print)
Collection ISSN: 2156-8170 (electronic)

Cover design by Jonathan Pennell
Interior design by Exeter Premedia Services Private Ltd.,
Chennai, India

First edition: 2012

10 9 8 7 6 5 4 3 2 1

Printed in the United States of America.

For college deans past, present, and future who often do too much to achieve too little.

Copyright Acknowledgments

Abstract

The metaphor of dosage offers a rich organizing principle for managers. It focuses our efforts on such fundamental, pragmatic communication issues as amount, frequency, delivery system, sequencing, interaction with other agents, and contraindications. It suggests compelling new answers to fundamental problems that all managers must face, with an appreciation of basic issues beyond our conscious awareness. The book is targeted toward graduate, executive, and professional audiences.

In our day-to-day lives—whether we are discussing things with our housing contractor, our cable repair man, our doctor—we must constantly decide how much communication we should engage in to pursue our projects. This work focuses on the dosage metaphor as a way of confronting this question—what level of communication, both in terms of amount and of depth, is really necessary to accomplish particular purposes? Most communication theories implicitly paint a picture of the prevalence and paramount importance of communication, with a "communication metamyth" that more is necessarily better. This book provides the first truly comprehensive treatment of dosage. It also focuses on perhaps the most contemporaneously interesting issues of change and of productivity. The final chapter presents the dosage metaphor in broad sweep, suggesting a countervailing minimalist approach to communication.

Keywords

dosage, innovation, managers, managerial communication, managing relationships, match, metaphors, organizational change, productivity

Contents

List of Tables and Figures

Tables

Figure

List of Boxes

Preface

I have been a practicing manager for nearly two decades in a number of different capacities: as a department chair, as a dean, as a noncommissioned officer in charge of the supply and services division of a hospital, and as a warehouse supervisor. I have also been conducting network analysis, innovation, and information behavior research for over three decades now. The combination of these experiences has led me to a central question: what level of communication is really necessary to accomplish particular purposes?

Most communication theories implicitly paint a picture of the prevalence and paramount importance of communication, through a "meta-myth" that more is necessarily better. However, in our rapidly expanding information society, there is increasing evidence that less communication actually may be better. Some reliable empirical studies indicate desired impacts resulting from much less communication than previously thought. In my own research I have often been surprised by the effectiveness of relatively low levels of communication, which I will detail in this work.

I came to a greater appreciation of these issues as a result of long-standing research programs in innovation, information seeking and media exposure, and network analysis. My first research paper focused on the normative level of communication activities in a range of organizational communication networks.[1] It demonstrated surprisingly low levels of communication, especially for innovation content. This is a finding that was again confirmed in my longitudinal research on innovation within the Cancer Information Service Research Consortium (CISRC), a somewhat unique virtual organization composed of researchers and practitioners. While communication has been viewed as central to innovation, surprisingly little communication occurred during the length of this project. The empirical work that has been done on actual communication behavior suggests that, especially for innovation-related communication in organizations, people do not talk to each other very much.

Another program of research, which has now spanned nearly 30 years, grew out of my work in the Office of Research of the US Information Agency that focused on pragmatic concerns relating to the factors which lead to exposure to particular information carriers (e.g., magazines, films). This line of research has expanded to focus on more general issues related to information seeking summarized in my books *Information Seeking: An Organizational Dilemma*, *Cancer-Related Information Seeking*, and my more recent work with Donald Case *Health Information Seeking*. One of the major theoretical problems with traditional, functionalist explanations of structures has been a failure to incorporate a comprehensive perspective of individual action. A focus on individuals' information seeking embedded in communication structures has caused me to recognize the dosage issues embedded in such transactions.

Needless to say I draw on this prior work for some basic descriptions of the communication theories discussed here. However, following a classic narrative approach to literature reviews, I interweave these basic descriptions, with a focus on their significance for a dosage metaphor. I also use my recent overview essay[2] focusing on dosage as a bridging metaphor for theory and practice as a starting point for Chapters 1, 2, and 8.

In recent years communication research has shown a curious tendency to ignore fundamental issues critical to practice. This is certainly the case with productivity, effectiveness, and efficiency issues. Even more troubling, our comfortable shibboleths do not stand up to close empirical scrutiny. Most communication theories assume that more communication is better and imply high volumes are beneficial, but the few studies that have been done suggest, at best, complex contingencies and cost/benefit equations.

This work, then, is about uncovering a metaphor in use, making explicit how it enriches the practice of management, particularly in terms of understanding that more is not necessarily better. It is not about the study of metaphor qua metaphor, which has been the focus of extensive research in a variety of disciplines. Here I will argue that the metaphor of dosage offers us a rich perspective on communication, focusing our efforts on such fundamental, pragmatic communication issues as amount, frequency, sequencing, delivery system, interaction with other agents, and contraindications. It suggests compelling new research questions and answers to fundamental problems that all managers must face, with an appreciation of basic issues beyond our conscious awareness, thus providing a primer highlighting basic principles of managerial communication.

As Dean of the College of Communications and Information Studies for over a decade at the University of Kentucky, I jokingly referred to myself as the stealth dean, preferring a minimalist level of communication. As often as not I have seen other managers embroiled in needless difficulty from overdoing management. In many ways managers might be better guided by the old medical maximum of first do no harm, but, of course, US managers have a bias toward action.

Here, I seek to bridge both the world of practice and of research. Of course in doing so, I run the risk of pleasing no one. While it has become commonplace for scholars to apply metaphors to facilitate theory development, they are only haphazardly applied to practice. In spite of decades of research, we have at best only a fuzzy notion of what "dosage" is needed for specific effects. My desire here is to acquaint a range of readers with the underlying substantive and pragmatic issues related to the metaphor of dosage, providing readers with an analytic framework that can readily be applied to the everyday world of work.

My Thanks

I would like to thank Dr. Sally Johnson, who often has a different perspective on the arguments I present here, and my students in my introductory graduate communication theory class for reviewing earlier drafts of this work.

I would also like to thank David Parker, founding editor and publisher of Business Expert Press, and Debbie DuFrene, corporate communication collection editor, for their assistance and support.

Plan of Book

The first chapter has provided a framework for applying the basic principles of dosage to a manager's work. In the next chapter we focus on expanding the metaphor of dosage, detailing its many elements as well as discussing the use and limits of metaphor generally, and the history of the use of metaphor in organizational thought. These latter two sections, in particular, may be of only passing interest to the practicing manager.

Organizational communication has often explicitly used metaphors as a basis for its theoretic approaches. In Chapter 3 we focus on such basic organizational approaches as the right match between communication efforts and desired outcomes primarily reflected in communication channel research, differentiation and integration, and technology and structure. Chapter 4 focuses on managing relationships between two people in interpersonal communication, particularly in terms of compliance gaining in supervisor–subordinate relationships. Chapter 5 details the application of the dosage metaphor to the central managerial concern of productivity. Chapter 6 focuses on perhaps the most contemporaneously interesting issue of change. Here I highlight network analysis concepts such as the strength of weak ties, structural equivalence, and social contagion in the adoption and implementation of innovations. Chapter 7 turns to how an organization communicates with its publics, particularly in campaigns.

The final chapter discusses broader policy issues raised by application of the metaphor of dosage and the development of a minimalist approach to management. Managers must be ever sensitive to the issues of match and the possibility that overdoing communication can have as many bad outcomes as not paying enough attention to communication. How to achieve the right balance while minimizing their efforts, while still achieving the outcomes they desire, is perhaps the Holy Grail of management.

Prologue

Let us examine a common situation where a manager must increase his unit's sales. Unconsciously in most situations (consciously if the manager is a particularly good one) while those business goals are being determined, the manager must address the underlying communication dosage problems in deciding how best to impart critical information to his direct reports (Table 1).

We are all familiar with the elements that would be considered when a manager establishes immediate business goals. He will need to determine staging before specific tactics can be developed. If this is a new product, then the manager will need to do additional testing to determine the characteristics of the target audience and its needs. He will need to determine the following types of things:

- The amount of contact that should be acquired after the sale to ensure customer satisfaction.
- How frequently follow-up visits should be arranged and what their duration should be.
- Whether a visit should be in person or can be arranged by videoconferencing.
- Whether an image campaign is necessary to improve receptiveness of an audience before direct marketing can occur.
- If the content of the campaign interacts with other company campaign.
- If the company truly has the appropriate manufacturing capacity to produce a product.
- If a fast gear up will result in poor product quality.

Coincident with the manager's business decision-making, a set of decisions will also be reached relating to communication.[1] The manager may decide to set aside two separate, sequential appointments with key personnel to discuss thoroughly all of their marketing options. Alternatively, he might decide to give the client the recommended solution based on their initial marketing analysis, and then, after the client has had time

Table 1. Dosage in a Manager's Everyday Life

Dosage elements	Parallel elements	
	Manager's goals	Communication elements
Amount	Increasing sales	Duration of campaign
Frequency	Weekly goals for 2 months	Follow-ups
Delivery systems	Marketing strategies	Brochures MP3 Face-to-face meetings
Sequencing	Problem analysis, Implementation of solutions	Image campaign, then direct marketing, then mass advertising
Interactions	New product	Competitor's campaigns
Contraindications	Lack of capacity	Resistance to change, frustrating expectations
Dysfunctions	Poor quality	Client/customer pushback

to consider how the product might be used in their everyday work further testing to see if it is still a good fit; then to follow-up with a more lengthy detailed interview about additional product options. While this would be the preferred approach with most clients, managers might also consider traditional clients who don't handle change well and are usually frustrated by delays in product introduction (a contraindication), and that it would be best to have this sort of discussion with their manager rather than the end-user themselves.

For most clients, the manager then decides what communication channels would be the most appropriate to supplement face-to-face calls that deliver the initial sales pitch. He might decide to refer the client to a company website, to give them a manual, to show them a videotape, and so forth. Unfortunately, a manager may not know how the information provided might interact with other information sources the client is exposed to, such as coworkers, competitors, professional organizations, business analysts, the Internet, and so on. The manager also needs to be concerned with how this might impact clients more broadly. In this case, he might be worried about the client's business model, competitive situation, and general decline of their industry, and so on. In short, for their business strategy to be most effective, the manager needs to develop parallel elements relating to communication dosages to the one he follows more overtly for business ones.

CHAPTER 1

Introduction and Overview

Overview

As the prologue illustrates, in our everyday lives, when confronted with problems, we must decide how much effort we will engage in to achieve our ends. Managers must decide how much time they will expend to describe to workers the seriousness of potential layoffs; marketing directors must decide how much TV time they should buy, how frequently to sell a product; salesmen must decide when they have made enough arguments to close the deal, adapting their persuasive attempts to the level of resistance they sense in their audience; airline pilots must decide how much information they need to impart to their co-pilots to deal with emergencies; and skilled mechanics need to ensure that they get the right instrument for the next stage of their repairs. Fundamentally, in our day-to-day interactions with others, we must constantly confront issues of dosage.

In this work we will look at dosage as a metaphor that encapsulates fundamental principles that managers can use to guide their communication. When I have an ailment I go to a doctor for a diagnosis. The doctor evaluates my condition and then prescribes a treatment. If I am a good patient, I then exactly follow her prescription regarding the frequency, duration, and so on. But, unfortunately, we also know that people do not often comply with medical advice. They inadvertently skip doses, change treatment agents (often because of cost, the advice of their friends, or just reverting to habits), and they do not continue administration after the first signs that the immediate precipitating conditions have disappeared. All of these circumstances have direct analogs to the experiences of organizational consultants, change agents, and managers of internal communication campaigns (e.g., increasing workplace safety).

Fundamentally we must address the notion of what "dosage" is needed for particular effects. What volume, depth of communication, or both do we need to achieve particular purposes? Communication theories often implicitly paint a picture of the prevalence and paramount importance of communication. Systems theories point to the importance of coordination and interdependence, interpretive theories focus on sharing of perspectives in sense-making activities, discourse theories on the importance of dialog for collective action, and so on.

There is also what has been described as a "communication meta-myth" that more is better, with organizational members always desiring more communication, especially from formal channels, regardless of how much they are receiving,[1] interpersonal scholars historically argued that increased communication leads to "relational panacea,"[2] and uncertainty reduction has often been cast as a "direct and linear function of an objective quantity of information."[3] On the receiver's side there has been a concern with impacts of communication overloads, but there has not been concomitant interest in underloads and the, perhaps related, topic of ignorance.[4] As we will soon see, some partial, often implicit, attempts have been made to incorporate dosage, but not a synthetic approach.

The metaphor of dosage offers a rich organizing principle for managers in their everyday work. It focuses their efforts on such fundamental, pragmatic concerns as:

- amount
- frequency
- sequencing
- delivery system
- interaction with what other agents
- contraindications

It suggests compelling new answers to fundamental problems that all communicators must face, with an appreciation of some basic issues beyond conscious awareness. This is the ultimate hope for the more complete development of the dosage metaphor, that we look at some old problems, which are critical to any manager, with a new set of tools and vocabulary.

Dosage and Metaphor

All this suggests that a key question is *just what "dosage" is needed to achieve particular impacts.* "Simply proposing more or better communication is the oldest consulting recommendation in the book—and no one today really needs more meetings."[5]

What numbers of people and what amount of communication are needed to achieve threshold, critical mass effects, or both for the diffusion of innovations such as social media, for example? It may be the case for a number of innovations, minimalist communication strategies, involving some mediated communication and intense interpersonal communication involving only those immediately affected may be the best approach or, alternatively, perhaps a more viral marketing approach targeting opinion leaders.

Communication theorists tend not have measured approaches to problems. We do not know when to stop, and perhaps like a doctor who gives someone a drug because they expect one, in our consultant roles we are often pressed to do something. Unfortunately, however, too much communication is often associated with chaos, low morale, and inefficiency in organizations,[6] with information overload impeding effective communication,[7] and thus making groups less intelligent.[8]

The dosage metaphor offers an encompassing way of addressing these issues, particularly with an emphasis on the increasing importance of outcomes in this age of accountability. It focuses on the issue of how much should I give, how often, for how long, with an underlying appreciation for the darker side of effects (e.g., overdoses, allergic reactions, contraindications) as well. The dosage metaphor has rich implications, bridging us to persistent problems that managers face daily in implementing change.[9]

Seen as allegories or as figures of speech, metaphors may appear to be no more than simple literary or linguistic tools, yet there is far more to them than that. They are the outcome of the cognitive process that is in constant use—a process in which the literal meaning of the phrase or word is applied to the content in a figurative sense.[10]

Metaphors become a way of seeing and thinking; they provide a way of understanding one thing by appeal to another. They also reflect central issues of a particular time and place. They have been central to our thinking about organizations given their complexity. This was particularly so early on for issues related to productivity, efficiency, and effectiveness, seemingly the most rational of pursuits. Some of this early work in efficiency likened organizations to machines, while later work, more concerned with fit, match, and effectiveness, used more organismic metaphors.

Fundamentally, dosage refers to the administration of a therapeutic agent in prescribed amounts. Given its ubiquity in health disciplines, it is somewhat surprising that dosage has not been related in a more systematic way to communication. In part, this might be because of a presumed association with functionalist, post-positivistic explanations of behavior, and their concern with outcomes. Common definitions of dosage inherently have an element of administrative science that might be uncomfortable to some, in spite of the word's Greek root, which means *giving*. To those with a more simplistic understanding of modern medicine, dosage also seems to imply a denial of the particularistic, contextual, individualized focus of communication. However, the more modern movement to personalized medicine would seem to encapsulate many of the contemporary trends in communication as well. Just as a doctor knows that a therapeutic agent will not work for all people, a good communicologist knows that not all messages will have the same meaning for all people.[11]

Conclusion

There are several *key components* of a definition of dosage.

- First is the notion of an agent that promotes change.
- Second is the suggestion that the agent is therapeutic in some sense. Both of these components relate to the extensive use of the metaphor in the organization change literature. In a darker way, often a dose needs to be prescribed by an authoritative agent (e.g., doctor) before we can administer it

and it may have unintended or unknown side effects. It also
can be associated with agents of infection and with hard luck.

- Third is the relative strength, duration, and repetition of
the agent needed to achieve the desired effect. In medicine,
these factors are known with some precision because of
evidence.

In the next chapter we expand on these elements, highlighting their
importance for the practice of management.

CHAPTER 2

Definition and the Use of Metaphor

Metaphors provide a way of understanding one thing by appeal to another.[1]

> They are here, there, and everywhere. They run right through our language. They are used to make sense of the situations we find ourselves in. They shape our perceptions and can influence our attitudes and behavior. Metaphors are, to quote Morgan, "*a way of thinking* and *a way of seeing* ...".[2]

Metaphors enable us to apply our knowledge of a familiar subject, the base domain, to one that is relatively unknown, the target domain.[3] They become a way of both describing and evaluating action.[4] Metaphors can be generative because they may result in new knowledge about an unfamiliar terrain and new frames or perspectives for viewing social phenomena.[5] It is this generative sense that is the most useful because it can produce new insights by enabling us to see the world anew, facilitating our understanding of the phenomenon, and playful experimentation with a new phenomenon.[6,7]

While metaphors can be seen as very useful instrumental tools, they also stimulate us to play with ideas. They take what is well known and apply it to something else in a vivid and memorable way that has the potential of enhancing learning.[8] It has become commonplace for scholars to apply metaphors to facilitate theory development[9] and they have been particularly important in the field of communication.[10]

Metaphors are also frequently used by lay people to describe and understand their life experiences. They have become taken-for-granted elements of our culture and, in this sense, have become "dead" metaphors, because they are commonplace and accepted they are unlikely to result in new insights.[11] It is my hope that dosage is a particularly "live" metaphor,[12] which through its application easily lends itself to further conceptual development.

Elaborating on the Dosage Metaphor

Dosage is derived from a Greek word which literally means the act of giving. In modern usage it is most *commonly thought of as the administration of a therapeutic agent in prescribed amounts.* We now turn to a deeper appreciation of how the various elements of the dosage metaphor can enrich our understanding of the varying concerns of managers. Here we elaborate on the elements of the dosage metaphor that focus on amount, frequency, sequencing, delivery systems, interactions, contraindications, and dysfunctions. These elements will organize our discussion of dosage throughout the remainder of this book.

Amount

The major downfall of the network approach is that they are such sparse social structures that it is difficult to see how they can account for what we observe.[13]

The classic approach to amount in communication can be found in the mass media exposure literature. Questions of amount, repetition, and mode of delivery are central to communication campaigns and more generally media effects.[14] But in some ways this is equivalent to the very crude relationships between nutrition and certain health impacts. Foods may contain very healthy individual ingredients, and simultaneously contain some very unhealthy ones, as in the case of red wines, where some ingredients may be beneficial, but alcohol by itself can have numerous harmful impacts. Because I like a particular food I may accidentally ingest some elements that are healthy for me, but I do not necessarily do so knowingly. This also may be a very wasteful way of accomplishing a particular end that might be more directly served by taking vitamins.

One of the reasons this is so crude in the exposure literature is we do not often know whether people are paying attention[15]—absorbing the dose—or whether the body's immune system is actively fighting the dose, as in the Sherif's latitude of rejection notions which focus on the communication messages that are likely to be persuasive.[16] In chemotherapy the key challenge for oncologists is to figure out what is the appropriate level of poison with which the person can physiologically and psychologically cope. These issues also relate to notions of "drug receptors" and differential absorption rates of different organs (units in an organization[17]) and notions of absorptive capacity that we will discuss in more detail in a later chapter that focuses on change.

Communication literature is often unclear as to what the precise "dosage" is and how often it needs to be applied. Thus, "an indiscriminate increase in connectedness can be a drag on productivity, as people get bogged down in maintaining all their relationships."[18] Acquiring more information can result in delays and increase costs,[19] and too much self-disclosure can act to drive people away.

Frequency

One of the earliest shibboleths of communication theory is that repeated messages are more likely to have an impact. This again has direct analogies to medicinal dosages. We don't take one huge dose of a medicine and expect it to last forever. Rather, for the effect to be maintained it needs to be repeated over time, while we also may not be able to tolerate huge dosages, but need to gradually accrete certain impacts. Again, we have focused little on issues of absorption rates, even though March has provided compelling arguments that they are critical to organizational learning and ultimate survival. There also is the related issue of the rates of elimination of certain doses.[20]

But repetition can lead to bad outcomes, just as in the building up of drug tolerances and overdoses because of the lack of flushing of drugs. In structural research, it is well known that highly redundant linkages can impair creativity, in part, because group members have the same knowledge base that results in similar world views and conformity pressures. Nonredundant linkages have often been associated with weak ties and the spread of novel information in social systems. Similarly, more information can often undermine effective decision-making and, counterintuitively, in competitive information markets, the less information provided by a supplier the more likely this source was used again, in part because they developed a reputation for quality and focus.[21]

Sequencing

At times the sequencing of dosages is also important, as in chemotherapy, with gradually increasing doses of different composition as one's tolerance builds. This is somewhat akin to the pathways people follow in acquiring information[22] because the sequencing of questions may be particularly important for uncertainty reduction.[23] I might start a search for prevention information with a decision to consult a mediated communication channel, but I also may decide that I want this channel to contain authoritative information as well as a personal touch. This unique hybrid of properties is represented by my local service provider. After placing a call I might decide that a particular customer service agent is inexperienced, so I might then decide to try the web. I evaluate the new source as more credible, partially because of the nature of the messages that are being transmitted to me. While I can accept the site's message concerning the need for virus protection, I consider the linkage it is suggesting between RSS feeds and security breaches to be far-fetched and discount it. However, we also know that the pathways people follow and who they are exposed to in their information fields shape their interpretations and determine the answers they obtain and whether or not they obtain them efficiently and on time, if at all. The ordering of communication events, just as in the ordering of certain drugs, can produce unique impacts.[24]

Delivery Systems

The means of administration of a particular dose can also directly determine its impact. Some drugs are best taken intravenously, others can be taken in pill form, while still others can be inhaled. This is analogous to channel impacts in communication. Communication campaigns often are very strategic in their selection of particular channels, with a well-established maxim that the mass media are best at providing information while interpersonal channels are often crucial in persuasive efforts. Channel, or media, selection models in organizations have captured widespread attention. One of the major reasons for this interest is the assumption that there is an optimal match between channels and organizational tasks that leads to more effective performance, a traditional theme in communication research, a topic we will return to in much more detail in the next chapter when we cover media richness approaches.

Interactions

As we all know from the seemingly daily news coverage, drugs can have a number of interactions, both positive and negative, as well as contraindications. So, we discover the allergy medicine Seldane, for instance, interacts in dangerous ways with grapefruit of all things. We are instructed to take a drug with food, before eating, after eating, to not take it with other drugs, and to not drive while taking it because of its side effects. These issues can become another way of portraying the effects of context. So, for example, when the source and receiver share common meanings, beliefs, attitudes, values, and a mutual language, communication is more likely to be effective[25] with advances in proteomics increasingly specifying the compatibility of drugs and patients. Although, somewhat similar to communication, genomic medicine has proven to be much more difficult to achieve in practice than it is in principle.[26]

An example of dosage from innovation research suggests that when an innovation has a high level of perceived relative advantage and acceptance, a mediated communication strategy is perhaps most appropriate. The use of mediated channels as delivery systems, such as company newsletters, videos, magazines, and so on, may create an atmosphere of involvement and interest, producing a certain receptivity to organization-wide innovations.[33] Especially in situations where there is a highly motivated set of organizational members, the direct provision of information may be a highly effective strategy.[27] Alternatively, in the case of certain complex and risky information technologies, direct interpersonal communication and additional training may be necessary ingredients for successful innovation implementation.[28]

The concepts of match, fit, congruence, and contingency have been used rather loosely in the literature to capture an essential idea related to structures; there is some optimal arrangement of structural elements that promotes the accomplishment of particular functions, something we will cover in much more detail in Chapter 3. For example, Tushman found in an R&D laboratory that effectiveness is a function of matching communication patterns to the nature of a project's work, particularly at the subunit level.[29] Specifically, high-performing research projects need more intraproject communication than high performing technical service projects. Similarly, Kolb argued against the then faddish rejection of organizational status suggesting that structure provided a needed framework for team-centered, virtual organizations.[30]

Contraindications

A basic principle of pharmacology is that no drug produces a single effect. Thus, there are a number of conditions (e.g., being pregnant with the organizational analogy of spin-offs) in which a particular dose should not be administered. Contraindications go beyond interactions, then, by suggesting circumstances for which a dose should definitely not be applied. So a politician whose whole career is based on moral righteousness, should never knowingly transmit a duplicitous message. Jablin found that supervisors who desire open relationships with subordinates should never communicate negative relational information to them.[31] Similarly, violations of private self-disclosures to others can act to permanently damage interpersonal relationships.

Dysfunctions

Of course, as in all things, dosage also has a darker side. People can become too dependent on particular therapeutic agents leading to problems with withdrawal, addiction, and various forms of substance abuse. They also can believe more is necessarily better, leading to problems with overdoses and continuation of doses long after any benefit has occurred. These problems, in turn, can lead to resistance to the beneficial effects of therapeutic agents when they are truly needed, much like what has occurred with antibiotics and their over usage. At times, the wrong drug, such as high-powered antibiotics, can treat the symptoms but not the underlying cause of the disease. Similarly, universities, state governments, and other public agencies have persistent structural deficits attributable to profligate pension programs and fringe benefit packages, which are masked by stimulus packages and tuition increases. We have also seen in very competitive situations people who risk substantial long-term issues with their health to inject themselves with performance-enhancing drugs of various sorts. Just as in highly publicized cases of celebrity doctors, we have consultants who are likely to prescribe whatever the patient ordered, such as justifying higher compensation packages for chief executives.

A Brief History of Metaphor in Organizational Thought

Metaphors have dominated organizational thought from its very beginnings. This is in part because organizations are so complex that people need easily understood handles to begin thinking of them. In this chapter we will discuss the use of metaphor in organizations by first briefly tracing its history. The very term *organization* is derived from the Greek word for tool or instrument.[32] The use of metaphor in organizational theory dates back to its most elemental foundations and has been going on for well over a century.[33] This usage often reflects larger trends in social thought and historical circumstances. Therefore, the earliest applications dealt with extensions of Darwin's work to the survival of organizations which was shortly followed by the application of machine metaphors to the operation of the organization reflecting the early industrial age. The organic and machine metaphors still remain the most conventionalized metaphors applied to organizations; so much so it is hard to think about organizations without appealing to them.[34]

The distinction between *mechanistic* and *organic* systems, as a way of thinking about organizational innovation (Table 2.1), was popularized by Burns and Stalker who contrasted them as polar forms in their study of electronic firms at a time of rapidly changing commercial circumstances in the early 1960s.[35] While traditionally the differences between these two metaphors have been stressed, they do share some basic similarities. In both of these metaphors, organizations are viewed as material processors that rely on systematic treatments to produce changed outputs, that require energy, and those that are bounded from their environments.[36]

Table 2.1. Comparing Machine and Organismic Metaphors

Element	Machine	Organismic
Management Role	Mechanic	Control center
Change Agent	Engineer	Physician
Components	Cogs	Irreplaceable
Adaptability	Parts upgradeable	Gradual evolution
Communication	Well-oiled	Coordination
Load	Minimized	Interdependence
Under	Wasteful	Potential imbalance
Over	Stressful	Hyperactivity
Sequencing	Top-down	Mutual interdependence
Delivery System	Written, Plan	Oral, Coordinating
Contraindications	Rapidly changing environment	Resource poor environment
Dysfunctions	Dehumanizing	Ignores Hierarchy

In the mechanical metaphor, the organization is primarily viewed as a machine with many shared characteristics of bureaucratic organizations.[37] Management's role in the organization is viewed as an engineer or operator of the machine. The organization is viewed as a system of interlocking parts where everything must operate like clockwork. Dysfunctions are revealed with statements like "throwing a wrench" into the works or we appear to be in the "wrong gear." Unfortunately workers can often be viewed as so many cogs in this machine, easily replaced when they wear down, break, or need to be upgraded. As in any technologically based metaphor, the organization itself can be replaced by a better functioning machine, just as its major components can.

Biologically based, or organismic, metaphors operate on two basic levels. The first views the organism as a whole and how it interacts with its larger environment. This approach inevitably incorporates aspects of Social Darwinism. It looks at the adaptability of the entire organization with such statements as we must grow or die. Often institutional views of organization rely on this metaphor.[38,39]

The second level examines the organization as one biological entity. In this approach the interaction of interdependent parts are critical for the organization (Table 2.1). Parts are not easily changed nor removed.[40] So on the one hand, the organization has a greater commitment to its employees, while they, on the other hand, cannot exist without the organization.[41] This logic also suggests that individuals aren't isolated, competing entities within an organization where their individualistic career and political needs often result in dysfunctional efforts in mechanical organizations. As in system perspectives, the interdependence of the parts determines the success of the entire organization. Burns and Stalker explicitly articulated this in what has come to be thought of as a network metaphor for the internal communication structure of the organization.[42] In many ways this metaphor is compatible, obviously, with the dosage metaphor because the dose of a therapeutic agent may bring the whole organization back into harmony. The role of the change agent is to determine the right medicine and the appropriate dosage.

In recent years a host of other metaphors, often with more specialized applications, have also been applied to organizations including the notion of organizations as text with managers learning to read them,[43] theater,[44] puppet theater,[45] psychic prison,[46] garbage cans,[47] loosely coupled,[48] computers,[49] coach,[50] markets, game/teams, jamming,[51] voice,[52] discourse,[53] courtship in corporate mergers,[54] rooms,[55] herding cats.[56] Morgan's[57] very influential book, *Images of Organization*, presented a range of metaphors and was in turn metaphorically criticized for representing a supermarket of static ideas that could be pulled off the shelf like so many commodities.[58]

More recently, metaphors such as the panopticon have focused on the concerns of critical scholars and their focus on the constricting nature of organizational life, hegemony, and domination. Indeed, metaphors can become inextricably tied to the personal identity of organizational members.[59] In their seminal work on the American college president, Cohen and March describe eight metaphors of university governance: competitive market, administrative, collective bargaining, democratic, consensus, anarchy, independent judiciary, and plebiscitary autocracy.[60] More recently, constitutive approaches to organizations have been used by the Montreal school[61] to suggest that interactions are like tiles, and each one is connected to others, until in a bottom–up process where the whole organization edifice is socially constructed by imbrication.[62] Putnam and her colleagues have even gone so far as to classify organizational communication theory into four dominant metaphors: conduit, lens, linkage, and symbol.[63]

The conduit metaphor was particularly popular, at least implicitly, in early thinking about organizational communication. This metaphor permeates how the English language describes various communication processes describing the channels in which it resides and how messages are transmitted. It has subsequently been roundly panned by various critics,[64] in part because of its linkage to instrumental views of communication and administrative science encouraging a view that communication is the grounds and not the figure, or object, of metaphors.[65] More contemporary usage of this metaphor have discussed spillover effects and leakages of ideas outside of the containers they are in, producing important consequences for organizational innovation.[66]

For particular structural features of organizations, even more specialized metaphors have been applied such as skeletons and nervous systems. As with skeletons, the existing structure of an organization limits what is possible, if only by inertia, and at times quite formally. Geertz's spider web metaphor, which is often drawn in studies of organizational culture may also be quite appropriate here.[67,68] Spider webs both constrains and enables action. A spider, like an individual in a network, can make new strands in a web to meet new needs—but until it does there are some things it won't be able to do, as the web constitutes a real boundary to action,[69] just as metaphors have often bounded our thinking about organizations.

The Limits of Metaphor

Arguments over the use of metaphors are pointless: they are so pervasive and elemental to human thought that some see the use of metaphors as inevitable. As with any tool, however, a good craftsman needs to be aware of its limitations and whether another tool might be more appropriate in a particular application. The *central issue* of this work is *how does the metaphor of dosage helps us to understand communication in the workplace.* In this section I discuss some of the limitations of metaphor and some of the pitfalls of their use.

For a scientist, the ultimate hope in the development of any metaphor is to specify potential new lines for theory and for empirical research.[70]

In fact, with its roots in Aristotle, metaphor and comparison have been traditional tools of communication.[71] There has been some controversy over the extent to which the application of metaphor can truly move beyond comparison and correspondence[72] to a more creative, emergent, near dialogic view.[73] Dialog, feedback from application of metaphor, and resulting anomalous comparisons, can extend our understanding of both the metaphor and the situation to which it is applied. To be useful, a metaphor must involve objects of comparison that are at some distance from each other to offer unique and meaningful insights, emanating in part from surprise. The common usages of the dosage metaphor in organizations often apply to the darker side of organizational life: adopting a "poison pill" strategy to prevent corporate takeovers, giving someone a dose of their own medicine (or just a dose), and so on. But the degree of distance is also a source of tension because of potentially inherent residual dissimilarities.

The value of a metaphor, like the value of contrasting theories which never themselves comprehensively map onto all aspects of a phenomenon, is often in the eye of the beholder. Some can question its application in one or more particulars. So, doctors may not be in the same hierarchical position as managers in organizations, but they are in one, and the differences between the two can inform our understanding of both the practice of medicine and of management. It can also be argued that drugs are rather simply applied to very specific circumstances, but the emerging science of proteomics suggests that things are much more complex, that some medicines work best when we have detailed knowledge of the genetic receptivity of the "audience." Similarly, major theories of attitude change contrast the mindful rather than passive processing of messages as important for their ultimate efficacy, with a growing body of knowledge in positive psychology suggesting that some organizations may be more inclined to self-healing and resilience than others because of the "mindset" embodied in their culture. So, in playing off this overarching theme, many specific problems can be more readily understood and solutions emerge for them.

The most dangerous aspect of metaphors for many is that they may seriously mislead us in understanding of the phenomenon to which they are applied often through their latent entailments.[74] Thus, the container metaphor applied to communication often implies that the content of messages can easily be transported from a source to receiver. Embedded within them often are deeply held cultural and societal beliefs which is definitely seen in the fundamental application of biological, organismic, and mechanical metaphors to organizations and the manner in which the conduit metaphor permeates everyday language about communication. Perhaps the most fundamental value contained in the dosage metaphor relates to the seemingly taken for granted set of assumptions that there is a cure for any problem and that people actually want to be cured. Metaphors may serve to reify latent ideological positions and may actually, in a strange way, serve as an inertial force that protects organizations from critical inspection and resulting change.[75]

While metaphors potentially can liberate our thinking, suggesting new pathways for our theoretical work, one of their major limitations for members of social groups is their exclusionary potential. Metaphors can indeed privilege certain individuals. So individuals who have participated in team sports may have greater facility with the use of associated metaphors of teamwork in highly competitive organizational settings. For the dosage metaphor, those with a medical background and a more functionalist, administrative bent may be privileged.

One of the most interesting problems for a cultural approach is the presence of various subcultures within any larger social grouping. These subcultures are often associated with coalitions and political processes. Communication across subgroups is often difficult and subject to distortion because of the different language schemas, goal orientations, and task differentiations which become embodied in the metaphors they select and how they apply them.

Early approaches to culture tended to assume that there was one culture within an organization, or at least one dominant one, usually identified with management. Indeed, from this perspective culture becomes a variable management can manipulate for its own ends.[76] While comforting to management, this perspective vastly oversimplifies life in modern, complex organizations. In fact, some of the early classics of organizational research, such as the Hawthorne studies, involved the recognition of subcultures within organizations and how they resisted management imperatives.

The existence of multiple cultures and their configuration into coalitions can be taken as a given in most organizations. Perhaps the crucial question relates to whether or not there is a dominant culture or more of a pluralistic arrangement of subcultures. The emergence of one form or another may be in part dependent on the duality of concerns related to collaboration and control.[77] The weighting on these dimensions can determine the extent of pluralism in an organization: with control associated with the emergence of dominant subcultures and collaboration associated with pluralism. While there have been countless studies on how dominant coalitions, particularly management, exert power and influence, there is not a similar wealth of research concerning how roughly equivalent coalitions relate to each other in more pluralistic organizations, particularly at deeper levels. One way in which subcultures may relate to each other at the deeper levels of culture is through the usage of metaphor.

Meyer's research on the use of metaphors related to coalitions in a hospital setting is very interesting in this regard.[78] He argues that in hospitals there are four dominant root metaphors which serve as decision-making models for different coalitions: organism (physicians), computation (administrators, government agencies), cybernetics (boards of directors), and pluralism (the interaction of major coalitions) (Table 2.2). In making decisions concerning medical equipment it is unlikely that one of these metaphors can totally dominate, what is needed is an overlap of

Table 2.2. Mingling Decision-Making Metaphors

	Clinical	**Fiscal**	**Political**	**Strategic**
Root Metaphor	Organism	Computation	Pluralism	Cybernetics
Values	Patient welfare	Fiscal stability	Assimilation of competing interests	Mission driven
Decision Structuring	Collegial	Procedures and programs	Issue coalitions	Long-range planning
Bases of Influence	Professional	Financial acuity	Status, Hierarchical, Resource scarcity	Credibility

Source: Adapted from Mingling decision-making metaphors by A. D. Meyer (1984). *Academy of Management Review*, 9, 6–17. Copyright 1984 by Academy of Management.

argument that can make symbolic sense in the context of more than one model. Thus coalitions are built on the overlap of symbol systems as well as relationships, the "big tent" in political systems (e.g., the New Deal, the Reagan Revolution) that can provide an encompassing framework for disparate groups.[79]

Hiemstra provides an interesting illustration of these points in his examination of changes in coalitions in response to the shared interpretations of subcultures of the term "information technology."[80] This term encompasses a variety of subterms and it can be said to be relatively ambiguous, at least in the sense that it is subject to multiple interpretations. In general, these interpretations relate to the impacts of information technologies in terms of speed, efficiency, communication changes, depersonalization, motivation, and revolution. Most interestingly symbol manipulation relating to information technologies reflected the changing status of various organizational groups. Thus clericals become word processing operators and skeptics (often older managers) are labeled as "old timers." A strong culture, or at least an encompassing one, would be one which provides a medium for interaction, metaphoric or symbolic, between diverse subcultures.

Conclusion

In summary, perhaps the most controversial aspect of the application of metaphor comes from its very playful nature and the resulting messiness.[81] Quantitatively oriented scientists often see metaphors as antithetical to the scientific enterprise. In some ways, then, the uses of dosage metaphor may be particularly ironic since fundamentally dosage deals with quantity. Metaphors cannot be easily measured nor can their fit to a particular problem be precisely quantified as in a statistical test.

Fundamentally metaphors are in the eyes of the beholder.

CHAPTER 3

The Idea of Match

We now turn to a central theme of this book—the issue of *match* or *how much is enough to accomplish specific purposes.* The idea of match is closely linked to contingency theories which sought more sophisticated approaches to determining the resources necessary for particular organizational ends. Here we focus on three classics of organizational thought: Woodward's extensive research relating to technology and structure, Lawrence and Lorsch's work on differentiation and integration, and Daft and Lengel's more recent work on media richness. These approaches also may be instructive for classic medicinal approaches to dosage, which are increasingly concerned with personalizing medicine based on attributes of receivers.

Match

Underlying the perspectives discussed in this chapter is the more general assumption that an organization's (or unit's) *effectiveness is determined by the match (or fit) between its features and its surrounding environment.* Similarly for medical dosage applications, there has been a focus on *effective dose* or *threshold dose—the smallest amount of a substance required to produce a measurable effect.* This represents the lower bound of the *dose–response* or exposure–response relationship used to describe the change in an organism caused by differing levels of exposure to doses after a certain length of time. A dose–response curve is a simple *X–Y* graph relating the magnitude of the stressor to the response of the receptor, the organism under study. At higher doses, undesired side effects appear and grow worse as the dosage increases; the stronger a particular dose, the steeper the curve.

The concepts of match, fit, congruence, and contingency have been used loosely in the literature to capture an essential idea; there is some optimal arrangement of structural elements that promotes the accomplishment of particular functions. The idea of match permeates most of the literature related to organizational outcomes and has become a cornerstone of organizational theory, partly in reaction to the overly simplistic focus of classical management theory, which sought to discover the *one* best way of doing things in organizations.[1] This notion has been applied to many organizational outcomes: the congruence between rules (both perceptual and actual) of the two parties in the supervisor–subordinate communication relationship and job satisfaction,[2] the relationship between organizational strategy and structure,[3] the match between communication structures and performance in small groups,[4] the ideal amount of time in the office for teleworkers[5] to name a few. In this section the idea of match will be explored in more detail in terms of the following: the relationship between technology and structure, the balance between differentiation and integration needed in different environmental circumstances, and media richness.

Technology and Structure

At the macro-organizational level a number of research programs have examined the linkage between formal organizational arrangements and technology. This research stream started with the classic work of Woodward, which also had implicit references to mechanistic and organismic metaphors.[6] Her research program was an attempt to discover whether the principles developed within classic organizational theory actually correlated with business success. It was carried out in the mid-1950s and focused on the division of responsibilities between line supervision and technical specialists in 100 manufacturing firms of varying sizes.[7] It was soon discovered that there was no one best span of control; there was indeed wide variation in these structural relationships. There also was no clear linkage between structural arrangements and outcomes. However, when her findings were grouped by the technical methods used in a particular industry, clearer patterns of organizational structure and the resulting tone of human relationships inside the firm emerged. Further she argued that *no principle of management was valid for all technologies.* Thus, this research program was instrumental in spurring the development of contingency approaches to organizational theory.

Eventually Woodward identified three major types of technology: unit, mass, and process.[8] Unit or small batch firms produce specialized products which require highly skilled labor (e.g., tailored suits) and relatedly, in today's terms, tacit knowledge. Mass, or large batch, production generates products that have many standardized components resting on explicit knowledge, such as the classic assembly line operations of automobile manufacturers. Process production involves continuous flow technologies, often associated with liquid gases and solid shapes, such as those found in chemical and refining firms.

The findings of Woodward's study of 100 firms in Great Britain indicated that several formal structural elements differed systematically across the three major types of technology (Table 3.1).[9] Thus, different technologies resulted in different kinds of demands on individuals and organizations that were directly linked to their structural arrangements:

- The number of authority levels increased with technological complexity as did the willingness to delegate authority.
- Span of control was highest for mass production with the median range of 41–50 workers per supervisor (with some firms as high as 81–90), the lowest was for process production with the median of 11–20.[10]
- Administrative intensity was highest for process production.
- Written communication was greater in mass production organizations than in small batch or process organizations; in contrast, verbal messages were more frequent in process production.
- Unit production required day-to-day communication to coordinate activities, while mass and process production systems did not, and further, such an approach would introduce inefficiencies in their operations.[11]
- Mass production appeared to have the most negative effect on human relations.

*Table 3.1. Woodward Findings**

Type	Hierarchal levels**	Span of control***	Delivery systems
Small batch	3	21–30	Verbal
Mass production	4	41–50	Written
Process production	6	11–20	Verbal

* Medians.
** Levels in a classic organizational chart.
*** Number of subordinates for each supervisor.
Derived from Woodward (1965).

Other technology studies have also focused on delivery system-related issues. For example, Simpson found that mechanization reduced the need for close supervision and vertical communication, since machines dictated the work pace for subordinates.[12] Mechanization correspondingly increased the need for horizontal communication among first-line foreman related to joint problem solving and coordinating the work. Randolph and Finch, more generally, have found that technological certainty decreased the proportion of vertical communication and increased horizontal communication.[13] Interestingly, in more white-collar settings, high levels of formalization and socialization to professions may minimize the need for direct, interpersonal communication.[14]

For Woodward the amount and frequency of communication associated with various structures is contingent on technology and associated workflow, respectively. (Table 3.2 summarizes the relationship between the organizational theories focused on in this chapter and the various dosage elements.) Workflow implies a sequence in communication activities. She has much to say about the efficacy and implications of both written and interpersonal delivery systems in her work. Given the amount of forethought and planning needed for mass production systems, it is understandable that they require the highest level of written communication. On the other hand, the close coordination required for unit production and its unique demands imply a high level of oral communication, findings that echo media richness approaches. An improper match between technology and communication can affect the tone of human relationships. So, for example, if classic prescriptions related to the span of control were followed in mass production settings there would be both

Table 3.2. Matching and the Dosage Metaphor

Dosage elements	Researchers		
	Woodward	Lawrence and Lorsch	Daft and Lengel
Amount	Contingent on technology	Contingent on uncertainty in environment	Implicitly driven by equivocality
Frequency	Contingent on workflow	Driven by integration needs	Implicitly driven by equivocality
Sequencing	Flow of work	Progression, growth	Depends on level of equivocality
Delivery systems	Written, verbal	Integrating mechanisms, simple code systems	Variety
Interactions	Technology	Conflict resolution strategy	Time interval, social presence
Contraindications	Improper match	Improper match	Improper match
Dysfunctions	Tone of human relationships, inefficiency	Wasted resources, inefficiency, increased conflict	Wasted resources, inefficiency, misunderstandings

tremendous inefficiencies, with up to ten times as many supervisors used than required by the work, and the resulting close supervision could negatively impact employee morale.

Differentiation and Integration

Differentiation refers to the tendency of organizations to divide into more and more groups so that they can specialize their labor, become more sophisticated, larger, and competitive. Unfortunately the differentiation of skills required by complex modern organizations makes it increasingly unlikely that differing functional specialties will have similarities in outlooks[15] which also means there are relatively simple explicit code systems (e.g., numbers) used to communicate across groups in contemporary organizations. As the organization becomes more and more divided into functional subgroups, a corresponding pressure arises to integrate all of these groups with common organizational goals. The principal mechanisms employed by traditional organizations to achieve integration have included line management structure, cross-organizational teams and committees, individual coordinators, coordinating departments,

*Table 3.3. Lawrence and Lorsch's Findings**

	Industry		
	Container	Food	Plastics
Differentiation**	5.7	8.0	10.7
Additional Integrating	None	Individual integrators	Integrating department
Mechanisms		Temporary cross-functional teams	Permanent teams

* Adapted from *Organization and Environment: Managing Differentiation and Integration* by P. R. Lawrence and J. W. Lorsch (1967). Boston, MA: Harvard Business School, p. 138. Copyright 1986 by President and Fellows of Harvard College.
** Average number of functional units.

and formalized plans and procedures, all of which communicatively link organizational groups together for the purposes of achieving coordination toward common organizational goals[16] (Table 3.3).

> The capacity of an organization to maintain a complex, highly interdependent pattern of activity is limited in part by its capacity to handle the communication required for coordination. The greater the *efficiency of communication* within the organization, the greater the tolerance for interdependence.[17]

As the classic differentiation and integration literature suggests, matching structural features to an organization's environment is a critical issue that also relates to dosage metaphors. Lawrence and Lorsch found too little attention to integrative mechanisms makes it unlikely that the "medicine" will have its desired effect and too much communication is at the very least inefficient and an "overdose" may have damaging effects (e.g., opportunity costs in other areas).[18] In pharmacology this is referred to as the *therapeutic index,* or the relative margin of safety before a dose produces toxic effects. So, as the organization becomes more and more divided into functional subgroups that have pronounced differences in cognitive and emotional orientation, a corresponding pressure arises to integrate all of these groups to ensure they collaborate to achieve the unity of effort needed to accomplish common organizational goals. They clearly placed their approach in the context of systems theory, which argues that the parts of any system need to be linked together to accomplish its overall goals.

Lawrence and Lorsch sought an answer to the "… fundamental question, *What kind of organization does it take to deal with various economic and market conditions?*"[19] What they found is that organizations that were the most successful matched their levels of differentiation and integration to their environments (Table 3.3). This provided essential empirical support for contingency theories as the pace of technological change in our society was picking up speed.

To answer their research questions, Lawrence and Lorsch did a comparative case study of competing organizations in several industries. Organizations in the container industry, which had the most stable environment, had the lowest level of differentiation represented by distinct formal units (nearly six departments) and only used three *integrating mechanisms* that are commonly associated with the core of any bureaucracy: direct managerial contact, managerial hierarchy, and the paper system. The food industry averaged eight units with the addition of individual integrators and temporary cross-functional teams as integrating mechanisms. Organizations in the plastics industry, which had the most competitive environment, had, in addition to these 3 integrating mechanisms, integrative departments and permanent cross-functional teams at different levels of management to integrate their nearly 11 departments.

Most interestingly, they found that organizations that *had too many integrating mechanisms* in the container industry were *lower performers*, because of increased conflict, delays, and waste of resources. Lawrence and Lorsch argued, "an indiscriminate increase in connectedness can be a drag on productivity, as people get bogged down in maintaining all their relationships."[20] Indeed, dense communication within organizations has been found to be related to low production, low morale, and an experience of chaos[21] and, fundamentally, the more time spent on integrating the less that can be spent on doing the work.[22]

Lawrence and Lorsch's differentiation and integration approach also has implicit linkages to dosage metaphor (Table 3.3). The amount of communication is contingent on the level of uncertainty in the environment. The greater the uncertainty, the greater the need to differentiate to match environmental forces, and the greater the frequency of communication required to integrate the organization. While not dealing with classic channels of communication explicitly, they do articulate specific types of integrating mechanisms (e.g., *ad hoc* committees) and suggest that as organizations become more complex they rely on simple code systems, such as numbers, to communicate across a variety of perspectives. Integration is a direct response to growth, resulting in a split into more and more diverse groups, suggesting a clear evolutionary sequence. From a congruence point of view, approaches to differentiation and integration also require successful conflict resolution strategies to be employed in organizations. While it became fashionable to add more and more integrative mechanisms, Lawrence and Lorsch make it clear that they may be contraindicated by the type of environment in which the organization finds itself. They, and subsequent researchers, suggest *that too much integration, which is implicitly communicative, wastes resources, results in efficiency, and has the potential for increasing conflict.*

Media Richness

The primary way in which delivery systems are addressed in organizational communication is in terms of communication channels. Channels have been variously defined as "an information transmission system"[23] or "... the means by which the message gets from the source to the receiver."[24] Relying on the metaphor of a person on one shore trying to reach another on the opposite shore, Berlo distinguishes between three senses in which channels are used "modes of encoding and decoding messages (boat docks), message–vehicles (boats), and vehicle–carriers (water)" (p. 64).[25] Here we will mainly stress the sense of channels as message–vehicles, the contrivances by which messages are delivered to an individual. Thus "... a channel is a medium, a carrier of messages."[26]

General properties of channels can impact an individual's evaluations of them. Mass-mediated channels tend to provide information about a fairly general nature with considerable efficiencies in reaching large audiences quickly with a message.[27] Interpersonal channels are viewed as more effective in reducing uncertainty because they provide social support, enhance confidence in suggested outcomes, and are more tailored to individual needs and questions because of their immediacy of feedback and the situation specificity of their communication.[28] For these reasons interpersonal channels are seen as more useful in presenting complex, serious information and are the most influential.

Channel, or media, selection models in organizations have captured considerable attention over the years.[29] One of the major reasons for the interest in this area is the *assumption that there is an optimal match between channels and organizational tasks which will lead to more effective organizational performance,*[30] a traditional theme in communication research.[31] Most of this research has focused on the technological attributes of channels, especially the cutting-edge electronic channels, which have received such labels as the "new media."[32] So, for example, Wright found that the amount of time spent in online support groups was associated with network size and satisfaction.[33] As a result of the presumed revolutionary impacts of these new information processing technologies on organizational life, several major theoretical approaches have emerged to explain the underlying bases for channel selection.

Because *interpersonal* communication uses all of the senses, has immediate feedback, and is more spontaneous, it has become the *gold standard* against which other channels are evaluated.[34] This emphasis on face-to-face communication is related to the notion of *social presence* of a particular medium. Social presence refers to the degree to which a channel approximates the personal characteristics of face-to-face interaction[35] and has its roots in the work of Short, Williams, and Christie on teleconferencing.[36] Social presence approaches generally argue that mediated channels filter out nonverbal cues that make more salient the presence of other interactants[37]and thus reducing the impact of therapeutic agents. Social presence has been found to predict the perceived utility of media by managers,[38] and it is generally accepted that people will be most receptive to communication channels that reveal the presence of others.[39]

Researchers concerned with technological impacts on communication have come to classify both social presence arguments and media richness as two representatives of the media characteristics school.[40] These approaches assume that individuals make rational decisions concerning the most appropriate medium for any one particular communication task.[41] In general, it has been argued that complex, nonroutine tasks require more information processing than simple, routine tasks.[42] As task uncertainty increases, more personal, "rich" forms of communication substitute for more impersonal modes.[43]

Perhaps the most influential theory in this area is that of *media richness* as put forward by Daft and Lengel in their classic 1986 article that appeared in *Management Science*. This article started out with the question of "Why do organizations process information?" Media richness approaches argue that information processing requirements are a function of equivocality and/or uncertainty, terms that are frequently used interchangeably in the literature. To Daft and Lengel, equivocality added a twist suggesting that information stimulus may have several different interpretations. The resulting equivocality required much give-and-take to arrive at an unambiguous answer. This is especially true for organizational decisions where there are marked differences among units and they need to interact together to accomplish a larger organizational goal. The challenge for managers, then, is to create through their design decisions, information processing mechanisms capable of coping with an unclear environment. As equivocality increases, more personal, "rich" forms of communication are sought to substitute for more impersonal modes[44] thus highlighting match issues.

Communication media or channels differ in their inherent capacity to process rich information. "Information richness is defined as the ability of information to change understanding within a time interval."[45] Thus, media of low richness (e.g., impersonal written documents) are effective for processing well-understood messages and standardized data, while media of high richness (e.g., face-to-face meetings) are necessary to process information high in equivocality. So, individuals will ultimately choose channels which match the level of uncertainty reduction they feel is required in any one information processing task,[46] another way of saying the dose they need to achieve a particular effect. If a problem is extremely complex, then face-to-face discussions may be the only effective delivery system.

In summary, needless to say, Daft and Lengel's approach to media richness is not as grand in scope as the two preceding theoretical approaches to contingency. It operates as a classic theory of the middle range, clearly focused on one issue—media selection. As a result, its treatments of elements of the dosage metaphor are sometimes implicit (Table 4.2). This is particularly true for amount and frequency, which they imply would be determined by the level of equivocality. Obviously, the major strengths of this approach lie in its explicit means of explaining the appropriateness of particular delivery systems. The choice of media also interacts with the time interval available and social presence. The use of particular media may be contraindicated if it is an improper match to the level of equivocality represented by any one particular organizational task. *An improper match between equivocality and media selection wastes resources, results in inefficiency, and has the potential for increasing misunderstandings.*

Conclusion

The ideas behind match and contingency directly confront the communication metamyth that more is necessarily better. *Too much communication wastes resources, results in inefficiency, increases misunderstandings and distortions, leads to errors, and increases the potential for conflict.* Often a minimalist approach to management will produce better results with considerably less effort.

CHAPTER 4

Managing Relationships

While a manager has to be concerned about many types of interpersonal relationships in an organization, clearly the most important one to be managed is that of *the supervisor–subordinate communication relationship* (SSCR). Accordingly this will be the focus of this chapter, although reference will be made to managing other relationships such as those with coworkers. Managing interpersonal communication relationships dwells on issues that directly relate to the dosage metaphor, including compliance gaining and questions of intimacy and boundaries which focus on how much do I reveal to the other.

Interpersonal approaches often stem from commonly used metaphors (e.g., the depths of a relationship, dominance themes, exchange, boundaries). For example, the source metaphor of journey has often been used to describe the end point of the course of interpersonal relationships (Table 4.1). So you have travelers, with managers serving as guides/mentors; the events in the relationship; the progress made (expressed as the distance covered and perhaps the number of different places visited associated with the development of wisdom); the overcoming of obstacles; forks in the road describing the choices of different points of the relationship; the duration of the relationship; and ultimately the destination desired in the relationship.

General Properties of Relationships

Relationships can be characterized in a number of different ways. In this section we will describe the general properties of them typically focused on in network analysis. "A relation is not an intrinsic characteristic of either party taken in isolation, but is an emergent property of the connection or linkage between units of observation."[1] There are two primary types of relationships. *Contextually determined relationships* are associated

Table 4.1. The Journey Metaphor

Source metaphor journey	Target metaphor superior–subordinate communication relationships
Travelers	Guides
Vehicle	SSCR relationship itself
Journey	Events in the relationship
Distance covered	Progress made
Obstacles encountered	Difficulties experienced
Decisions about which way to go	Choices about what to do
Destination	Goals of the relationship

SSCR, supervisor–subordinate communication relationship.
Adapted from *Metaphor: A Practical Introduction* by Kovecses, Z. (2002). New York: Oxford University Press, p. 7.
Copyright 2002 by Zoltan Kovecses. Reprinted with permission of Oxford University Press, Inc.

with situationally or culturally determined roles. For example, Katz and Kahn viewed organizations as "fish nets" of interrelated offices, and this is particularly important for SSCR.[2] Contextual properties are intimately associated with asymmetry. Essentially asymmetry means that a relationship is not the same for both parties. This is an important network property because there are a multitude of differences between organizational members, especially in terms of status and the direction of communication. Thus power/dependence relationships are an especially important class of asymmetric relationships.[3]

Actor-determined relationships reflect the idiosyncratic bondings that characterize relationships between particular interactants. For example, importance, a variable that has traditionally been examined in network studies,[4] provides a direct assessment of the tie between an informal communication relationship and work performance. It can be associated with the more abstract concept of work dependency which relates fundamentally to the degree of access individuals have to needed task-related information.[5] Often individuals in networks come to rely on their peers for work-related advice. These peers are not formally assigned by the organization, but rather these relationships develop more informally, often as a result of friendships.

Reciprocity refers to whether or not both parties to a relationship characterize it in the same way. Reciprocity has been directly related to such substantive processes as selective perception and selective attention or the total volume of communication in an organization. For example, often a supervisor will not be as aware of relationships with workers as they are of the relationships with his/her bosses. So when asked with whom they communicate they will forget about a worker, but the worker will remember his/her relationship with the boss. This linkage is therefore unreciprocated; the worker believes it exists, but the manager does not[6] (Box 4.1).

Box 4.1
Seeking Information on Superior's Expectations

A persistent problem, especially for newcomers who are often deluged with information and highly uncertain about what they should do, is finding out their superior's expectations. Over the last couple of decades substantial research streams have focused on this problem in the organizational behavior and communication literatures. These streams have highlighted the importance of feedback seeking for a new employee's socialization, job performance, and ultimately turnover.[7] They have also identified a number of tactics employed as well as barriers to finding information.[8]

In terms of the elements of the dosage metaphor one consistent problem for amount and frequency is the issue of face. If one asks questions too often on too many subjects, they run the risk of forming an impression that they really do not understand their job and they have misunderstood what the boss really meant by an "open door."

Sequencing is also important. It may be more readily understood if one has questions at the onset of her job rather than later. She can also use a sequence of sources starting with those more remote from the supervisor before directly approaching the boss, which leads to the topic of delivery systems.

For delivery systems new employees can turn to a company's intranet site which has advantages for them of avoiding asking too many questions from people who may form erroneous impressions of them as well as the opportunity to consult as often as needed, often

(Continued)

(*Continued*)

anonymously. A subordinate can also ask a number of third parties, including coworkers, parceling out to a variety of others their concerns and thereby diminishing the risk of bad impressions. Some organizational cultures are highly competitive and place a paramount importance on autonomous performance. If one asks direct questions of their peers in these cultures, they run the risk of ridicule and violations of privacy boundaries when this information is strategically shared with others by someone who was mistakenly trusted.

Thus, some strategies run the risk of dysfunctional consequences. Third parties can offer bad advice. A supervisor may enjoy being a mentor and start wondering why the new employee does not ask questions directly. Perhaps the most interesting dysfunctional consequence stems from issues of status. In Blau's classic studies on advice seeking in a government office, he discovered that high-status individuals shared expertise readily with each other with the expectation it would be reciprocated, but that low-status people, who could not reciprocate in kind, were often spurned.[9] They often ended up sharing bad information with their other low-status peers. However, this pattern might be avoided by multiplex relations—one in which you seek advice on one dimension while giving it in another. In these situations, status interacts with a need for information to determine the overall pattern of advice seeking.

An important general property of a link is its strength with direct analogies to dosage. Typically the frequency of communication is used to indicate the strength of a link;[10] however, there are many possible indicants of the strength, each of which has different implications for dosage. For example, wide-ranging contacts of short duration may indicate individuals are searching for potential sources, while a few focused contacts of long duration may indicate the development of tacit meanings.

Another way of characterizing relationships, one that allows complex simulations of the spread of information and the development of social systems, is in terms of a few simple interaction rules that govern their development into self-organizing systems. So the susceptibility of a node to infection (usually a disease, but sometimes a new idea) spreads through

direct contact with others represented by threshold rules and how connected the system is (strong cliques inoculate against the spread of new
ideas) can determine the extent of information cascades,[11] something we
will return to when we discuss change.

Multiplexity refers to the nature of overlap, or correspondence,
between differing networks (e.g., friendship as opposed to work). The
nature of these overlaps is of great pragmatic concern, because it can suggest the inherent capabilities of individual actors within systems, and it
also has rich implications for the understanding of social systems generally. Organizations are actually composed of a variety of overlapping and
interrelated networks of differing functions;[12] however, functional dimensions are but one of the many dimensions along which network linkages can be multiplexed.[13] At its heart, multiplexity refers to the extent to
which different types of network relationships overlap: "The relation of
one person to another is multiplex to the extent that there is more than
one type of relation between the first person and the second."[14]

The degree of multiplexity has been related to such issues as the intimacy of relationships, temporal stability of relationships, reduction of
uncertainty, status, the degree of control of a clique over its members,
performance, redundancy of channels, and the diffusion of information.[15]
Multiplexity is also crucial to processes of social contagion, because it can
be expected that individuals with a high degree of participation across different types of networks might be more affected by contagion processes,
such as the dissemination of knowledge, than those individuals involved
in only one type of network.[16]

Hartman and Johnson examined the relationship between multiplexity and role ambiguity and commitment.[17] They found direct associations
between functional networks and these concepts. Role ambiguity was
most directly linked to conflicting information or perceptions of roles,
and thus it is most closely linked to the uniplex network relating to job
duties. On the other hand, commitment was most directly tied to organizational goals. In addition, the other functional networks of satisfaction
and nonwork impacted on commitment. As a result, the multiplex combination of these network properties had more of an impact on commitment than they had for role ambiguity. The overall pattern of their results
stresses the importance of carefully considering the nature of multiplex

networks with dimensions of multiplexity in some ways acting as if they were therapeutic agents.

The strength of weak ties is perhaps the most well-known concept related to network analysis. It refers to our less-developed relationships that are more limited in space, place, time, and depth of emotional bonds. Weak ties notions are derived from research on how people acquire information related to potential jobs.[18] It turns out that the most useful information comes from individuals in a person's extended networks—casual acquaintances and friends of friends. This information is the most useful precisely because it comes from infrequent or weak contacts. These weak ties are most often bridges that link different social worlds. So, weak ties are also crucial to integrating larger social systems, especially in terms of the nature of communication linkages between disparate groups.[19] Granovetter now maintains that this bridging function between different groups is a limiting condition necessary for the effects of weak ties to be evidenced.[20] Weak ties, however, may be discouraged in organizations because of concerns over loyalty to one's immediate work unit and questions of control of organizational members. Strong ties may also be preferred because they are more likely to be stable and because, as a result of the depth of their relationship, individuals may be willing to delay immediate gratifications from the other person associated with equity demands.[21] Individuals to whom an individual is strongly tied may also be more readily accessible and more willing to be of assistance.[22] Strong ties are also essential for the sharing of tacit knowledge.

Relationships as Exchanges

The exchange metaphor has been a central theoretical starting point for many interpersonal communication theories and may be the most popular modern framework for describing the overall properties of a relationship.[23] For example, equity in emotional exchanges has been seen as a cornerstone of relational maintenance with both parties giving and receiving equal value in their relative dosages.[24] As Bellah and others point out, the underlying cultural value of Lockean individualism is also dominant in our larger cultural frame. In this view individuals are seen as driven to maximize rewards through their interaction with each other.[25] Basically, as defined by the Oxford English Dictionary, an exchange represents "the action, or an act of reciprocal giving and receiving."[26]

Obviously, an exchange relationship can rest on extremely rudimentary understandings of others, based on such fundamental issues as fair price and trust that the other party will follow through on bargains. Relationships are seen from a utilitarian perspective, with the primary bases for continued relationships resulting from a perception of mutual gain. For communication scholars often information exchanges are the critical focus.[27] However, exchange relationships, once started, develop assets in and of themselves, based on their start-up costs, which make it more likely they will continue and endure.[28]

Exchange relationships are often embedded in the more encompassing metaphor of markets. Markets, through the mechanisms of exchanges, operate to diffuse information rapidly to interested parties[29] in an overall configuration often cast as traders in a bazaar.[30] In focusing on exchanges, this approach provides a theoretical focus for the development of relationships between interactants who may otherwise lack compelling motives to interact. Indeed, we may seek exchanges with others because they are not like us and they have resources that we do not possess.

The nature of relationships is determined by notions inherent in exchange; achieving a fair price for a good or service. In pure market-exchange relationships the only thing that may matter is the value of the goods exchanged. In network-based exchanges, normative controls may also be operative in the relationship[31] and the consequences of untrustworthy behavior may cloud concurrent and future interactions,[32] with one interaction potentially harming all future ones. In fact, for people who are unscrupulous in their relationships, the possibility of their behavior being sanctioned internally provides a positive incentive to interact outside of their social system with members of other groups.

SSCRs

SSCRs are among the most common interpersonal relationships within organizations and many would argue it is the dyadic relationship of greatest importance because of its impact on productivity and on job satisfaction.[33] This relationship "is limited to those exchanges of information and influence between organizational members, at least one of whom has formal (as defined by official organizational sources) authority to direct and evaluate the activities of other organizational members."[34]

The SSCR plays a key role in many organizational processes as Table 4.2 reveals. This table classifies a selected list of these processes based on relationship type, work and nonwork relationships, particularly concerning affective (e.g., friendship) relationships, affiliative ones (e.g., political coalitions), or both, and the locus of impact of the relationship: either individual or organizational. This is a list of possible impacts; not all SSCR are going to impinge on all of these factors. Obviously the more cells a particular SSCR affects the more important it is for both the individuals involved and the organization, a different form of multiplexity. The SSCR is the only organizational dyadic relationship which has such far-reaching potential impacts. Most other relationships are much simpler, being relatively easily categorized into one or another of the cells shown in Table 4.2.

Table 4.2. The Impact of Superior–Subordinate Communication Relationships on Other Organizational Processes

	Relational type	
Locus	**Affective/affiliative**	**Informational/work**
Individual	*Cell 1*	*Cell 2*
	Social support	Information load
	Trust	Role ambiguity
	Satisfaction	Openness
Organizational	*Cell 3*	*Cell 4*
	Integration	Coordination
	Commitment	Control
	Coalition formation	Innovation

Cell 1 reveals a combination of affiliative/affective impacts whose primary locus is the individual. Variables such as social support, trust, and satisfaction would be included in this cell. The SSCR can mediate these processes for both parties. However, it must be remembered that while it is probably the most important relationship, it is only one relationship which may have such impacts.

Cell 3 indicates organizational level affective/affiliative outcomes. Here the locus is not the individual, but the emergent effect of this relationship on the organization. Effective SSCR can speed integration of individuals into ongoing organizational processes and commitment which diminishes turnover. However, on the darker side, supervisors can recruit subordinates into coalitions which contest for power and increase the level of conflict in an organization. Jablin found that supervisors who are perceived to be highly involved in politics are perceived to be less open, and their subordinates are less satisfied in general with these SSCRs.[35]

Cell 4 stresses the importance of SSCR in the systemic processes of coordination and control. Here the relationship becomes crucial in maintaining the organizational system. It is at this level that such factors as hierarchical distortion become so critical to organizational operations. Because the SSCR is the primary link in a hierarchical chain it has a determinant impact on whether or not long-linked chains become so distorted as to diminish the capacity of an organization to effectively coordinate and control its operations and to respond to innovative proposals.

Finally, in Cell 2, which contains individual informational/work processes, various impacts of the SSCR on such concepts as decision support, information load, and role ambiguity directly relate to dosage issues. In addition, the greater the semantic information distance, which often reveals differences in tacit understanding of work issues, the more problematic the SSCR. While it is commonly held that supervisors serve as a central source of information for employees, perhaps the most critical issue is the extent to which parties serve as unique sources of information for each other. It is here that such conventional issues in interpersonal communication as openness and privacy come to the fore.

Openness

If *self-disclosure* information about oneself is purposively communicated to the other it is openness. It can differ in depth and breadth which can be used to operationalize the degree of intimacy in a relationship. It contains elements that are unknown or unknowable to the other. Interest in self-disclosure has its roots in humanistic psychology and the ideology of honest communication[36] with a cultural myth suggesting that increased openness is helpful for relationships,[37] a view which has been increasingly met with skepticism.[38] "In fact, there is abundant evidence that long-term relationships are maintained by illusions of truth, exaggerations of goodness ..., and less than full communication."[39] The classic view of self-disclosure, however, asserts that interpersonal and personal understandings occur through self-disclosure, feedback, and sensitivity to others. In this view, the ideal interpersonal relationship is one in which both parties allow the other to fully and openly experience each other.

Generally research in this area started with the hypothesis that disclosure leads to liking, attraction, and positive perceptions of the other's character. Such communication permits the continued growth of the individual. The intimacy of relationships between us increases if communication is of this particular kind.[40] Generally four dimensions of disclosure have been identified,[41] all with parallels to the dosage metaphor:

- breadth, or the number of topics
- depth, or the intimacy of the content
- duration
- valence, whether the disclosure is positive or negative

Clear norms exist as to the amount of reciprocity suggesting that if one shares a certain amount and kind of information the listener needs to reciprocate to complete the exchange. Further, it is suggested that the reduced likelihood that the other will share information outside of the dyad disclosed to them by the other results in greater disclosure.[42] There also needs to be a recognition of the time and energy that a truly intimate relationship involves.[43] Thus, there are fundamental similarities in the dosage metaphor and truly interpersonal relationships.

As Bochner has pointed out, inappropriate self-disclosures can actually produce negative impressions and people may be reluctant to self-disclose for fear it might damage their relationships, indicating a sensitivity to side effects for this "therapeutic agent."[44] Research in this area has resulted in a growing appreciation for the many dysfunctional aspects of self-disclosure and circumstances where it is contraindicated. So research findings have indicated very *highly disclosive* individuals are judged to be[45]

- less intelligent
- less well adjusted
- less likable

Self-disclosure can obviously have many benefits including catharsis, maintenance of positive relationships, validating self-concepts, bringing a sense of cohesion, fulfilling ethical obligations, greater social influence, securing social support, and so on. However, it also can have many dysfunctional consequences including potential loss of relationship depending on content reaction of others, loss of self-concept and esteem, privacy violations on the part of the other, loss of influence and face, and inflicting harm on the other.

In addition, sometimes people feel freer because of their social contexts to be more intimate with strangers, with those with whom they have weak ties, because there are fewer repercussions than with close acquaintances and friends. It also has been suggested that openness plays a more equivocal role in relational maintenance with findings suggesting an inversely negative relationship after controlling for such factors as positivity.[46] Accordingly, the initially optimistic vision has been replaced by and large by a more *strategic one that suggests that the disclosure of information be selective, with more positive contents*. Interestingly, married partners frequently engage in less openness than those engaged to be married or seriously dating. Only a very small percentage of communication with others, even our intimates, is truly disclosive. This appreciation has resulted in a renewed interest in privacy and the boundaries of self-disclosure.

How Much Do I Reveal? When?

One of the fundamental issues in interpersonal communication relates to how open one is with the other and the degree of self-disclosure one engages in (which often rests on reciprocal exchanges). In fact, many view this issue to be central to definitions of interpersonal communication.

It is also wrapped up in notions of privacy and boundaries in relationships. A central question in this regard is whether or not I can be open when all others in my environment are closed.

While this issue could be related to a variety of relational characteristics (e.g., trust and credibility) here we will return to openness, a variable which has received considerable attention in the literature[47] and which cuts across multiple levels of analysis.[48] In spite of the fact that openness is crucial to organizational effectiveness,[49] there is considerable evidence that subordinates are unwilling to be open in their SSCR,[50] with recent arguments that openness may not be beneficial in all circumstances, especially in terms of individual consequences.[51]

One of the central issues involved in whether or not relationships are open is that of proportion[52] which could be considered a form of dosage. If individuals enter the organization with an essentially open approach to their relationships with others, what factors can cause this approach to change? One factor which might lead to change is the experience of asymmetry; that is, some of the others, or alters in sociological terminology, with whom the person has relations act in a closed manner. Now the key issue is at what point does the perception of closed relationships cause an individual to change his/her own behavior? Does just one particularly devastating experience cause change, or is it likely that a substantial proportion of relationships with others has to be closed to lead to a negative reaction? Or are people more discriminating? Do they reciprocate and behave toward others as these others behave toward them? Do people have closed relationships with only those people with whom they are at risk (e.g., I want something from them or they can punish me in some way)?

Guardedness against change might dissipate over time if a certain level of trust has been established. While there has been much speculation concerning the relative time required to build an SSCR, not much research has been done to examine the temporal nature of the SSCR.[53] Are the parties in the dyad likely to be closed until they know the reactions of the other in some way, suggesting a sequential pattern of doses?

Issues of proportion, both of relationships and of prior experience, can have a substantial impact on SSCR. Naturally if a person has had consistently negative experience with superiors, or consistently positive ones, they can be expected to respond with less or more openness respectively. The really interesting issue is the point at which the individual tendency to react becomes more negative. Jablin's study, which examined the content of SSCR suggests that only a minimum amount of negative messages, especially those concerning the underlying relationship between the two parties, can act to close off an SSCR in some instances.[54] Jablin argued that reciprocal acceptance by both parties is crucial to an open relationship. The individual must perceive that both her messages and who she is as a person will be responded to positively before she will choose to be open. However, in an atmosphere of closed relationships, the individual may not feel that this essential precondition is being fulfilled. Thus subordinates are more likely to distort information when they perceive their supervisors are actively withholding information or are politically motivated.[55]

Some of the most compelling research findings in the social science literature in the last couple of decades are those related to the growing social isolation of Americans. Robert Putnam detailed in his book *Bowling Alone* the decline in membership in social groupings and the impacts this has on a larger sense of community.[56] Similarly, a series of studies on network analysis has detailed that Americans, on average, have very few people with whom they can share personal information with. In 1985, the General Social Survey asked a nationally representative sample of Americans how many confidants they had with whom they could discuss important matters. This survey was followed up in 2004, with depressing results: the number of people saying there was no one nearly tripled. The mean network size decreased by about a third, from around three in 1985 to around two in 2004. There were dramatic decreases in nonkin ties and fewer contacts in voluntary associations and neighborhoods. There also appears to be a pronounced tendency to have contacts with others like oneself.[57] All of this suggests that the sort of intimate, disclosive relationships that have historically been the "gold standard" of interpersonal communication are very much the exception, not the rule.

The amount of self-disclosure is generally considered to be an important indication of intimacy of a relationship. Discordant interpersonal relationships often stem from a lack of match between the degree of self-disclosure within a relationship and what both parties perceive as the stage of the relationship. Lack of trust in a partner may contraindicate a tendency to self-disclose. Classically there is also a key reciprocal component to self-disclosure. When one discloses something about oneself, it is expected that the other will also disclose similarly intimate topics.

Self-disclosure appears to be another example of curvilinear impacts and match issues that are directly related to the dosage metaphor.

Social Penetration Theory

Self-disclosure is perhaps the central concept in Altman and Taylor's *Social Penetration Theory*.[58] They argue social penetration gradually progresses during a relationship from superficial nonintimate areas to more intimate central areas. Relationships, therefore, can be characterized by both greater depth and breadth. Breadth frequency is determined by the number of different topical areas, breadth categories, open to another person, and the amount of interaction, in each of them. Rewards and cost, somewhat similar to exchange processes, often drive the development of social penetration processes within a relationship. Interestingly, more modern views, suggest that relational avoidance results from a direct linear function of relational closeness.[59]

Altman and Taylor identify *four stages* in a relationship, which echo some notions of sequencing of dosage levels:

- The orientation stage is characterized by stereotypes and superficial knowledge of the other.
- The exploratory affective exchange stage has some initial attempts at self-disclosure that one hopes will be reciprocated.
- The affective exchange deals with deeper more intimate areas central to the personality.
- During the stable exchange stage, people fully understand each other and communication is efficient.

Privacy

Sandra Petronio has been engaged in a decades long research program focusing on the boundaries of privacy.[60] Essentially she writes about the struggle of whether to tell or not to tell, with a subsidiary issue of how much to reveal. She asserts that people want to feel that they are the rightful owners of their personal information. Because there are risks to disclosure (e.g., disclosing at a bad time, telling too much about ourselves), people want to control how much information the other can receive, engaging in conscious risk assessments concerning the costs and benefits of sharing. On the other hand, as we have just seen there also are potential payoffs to disclosing private information to others especially in terms of enhanced intimacy. Once information is shared it becomes co-owned, with negotiated rights and responsibilities for both parties.

Petronio's *Communication Privacy Management* (CPM) theory consciously uses the metaphor of boundaries to illustrate the flow of private information to others.[61] *Five basic suppositions* underlay its rule management system:

- The focus is on private information.
- The boundary metaphor illustrates the demarcation between private information and public relationships.
- Concealing private information makes one feel vulnerable and relatedly people believe that private information is owned or co-owned by others.
- Decisions about boundary regulation are based on the rule management system.
- Privacy and disclosure are dialectic forces in relationships.

CPM suggests that not all disclosures of private information lead to intimacy. Many other factors are at play, one of which is frequency. Breaches of confidentiality, once information is disclosed and thus "co-owned" by the other may be one of the few situations where one dose, without repetition, can have lasting impacts.[62]

Compliance Gaining

Quite simply, compliance gaining represents attempts to get the other to do what you want and this may be the basic underlying factor in SSCR. One of the key issues in compliance gaining research involves the use of power: what amounts and types are necessary to achieve particular purposes. A key assumption of this approach is that of *match*—the idea that *you select particular tactics and strategies to fit a situation and one's desired outcomes.* Generally, these strategies can be employed to achieve compliance by manipulating consequences, using one's relational position, or by defining values and obligations.[63] This approach also implies that if one strategy appears not to be working, you should switch to another strategy, much as a supervisor would do with an employee who is consistently late for work. There also is, in an interesting way, concern for the relational consequences of compliance gaining attempts.

Compliance gaining has received considerable attention in interpersonal communication focusing often on typologies of strategies based on the seminal early work of Marwell and Schmitt.[64] It is heavily concerned with intentional, strategic approaches to managing relationships. These strategies, then, can be thought of as therapeutic agents chosen by the persuader. These strategies, or agents, may include the following:

- *Promising*, suggesting a reward will be forthcoming
- *Threatening*, suggesting a punishment will follow noncompliance
- *Showing expertise about positive outcomes*
- *Showing expertise about negative outcomes*
- *Liking*, exhibiting friendliness
- *Pregiving*, providing a reward before a compliance attempt
- *Applying aversive stimulus* until compliance is achieved
- *Calling in a debt*
- *Making moral appeals*
- *Attributing positive feelings* on the part of the other if they comply
- *Attributing negative feelings*
- *Positive altercasting*, people with good qualities comply
- *Negative altercasting*
- *Seeking altruistic compliance*, seeking compliance as a simple favor
- *Showing positive esteem*, saying the persona will be liked if they comply
- *Showing negative esteem*

A supervisor, then, has a wide range of potential strategies on hand that can be applied to achieve the level of compliance desired from a particular subordinate.

The Embeddedness of the SSCR

Even a cursory examination of the cells in Table 4.2 reveals that the SSCR is an important mediator of other organizational processes. Its relative importance is determined in part by its degree of embeddedness in the structure of communication relationships of an organization. This structure can constrain the parties in the relationship, limiting their range of action. Thus a supervisor's worst impulse for dominant behavior may be restricted by the rules governing his behavior.[65]

SSCR constitutes one of the few areas in the organizational communication literature which can be said to be relatively mature, with a well-developed body of research findings. Most of this literature examines relational states of the SSCR such as trust[66] and openness which we have just explored at length. The organizational communication structure within which these relationships are embedded is less frequently examined, but a subordinate is enmeshed in a web of relationships within which the subordinate can act to mediate any dose a supervisor might deliver.

Supervisors and subordinates move within a web of communication relationships, one of which is with each other. The relative strength of their relationships and the relative weaknesses of others may determine the extent to which they coact, a factor which has led some to argue that the importance of the SSCR has been overemphasized in the larger scheme of things.[67] Interestingly, Japanese managers deal with employees in a systemic manner (as part of an interrelated unit), while American managers treat employees as more of an isolated unit.[68]

Structure may determine the amount of redundancy in other relationships which can offset the harmful consequences of a bad SSCR. Often it seems forgotten that a supervisor naturally has relationships with multiple subordinates. So when a relationship with one subordinate turns sour the most likely outcome is that a supervisor will seek a more satisfactory relationship with another subordinate. Thus the easiest course for a supervisor is not to repair a relationship or to terminate it, but simply to let it wither.

A subordinate, on the other hand, has more difficulty in finding a qualitatively similar substitute, but through a patchwork of many relationships can recover many of the things that are lost from a poor SSCR. A bad SSCR is definitely not a good thing for the individuals involved or for the organization, but it need not be a devastating thing, because an individual's relative embeddedness in a larger institution provides alternative means for accomplishing various ends. Thus a series of uniplex relationships with persons other than the supervisor could substitute for a rich multiplex one.

On the other hand, a strong SSCR, one that cuts across multiple cells in Table 4.2, may actually hurt the organization in a number of ways. One finding from the interpersonal communication literature is telling in this regard. It has been found that as couples become more involved with each other, their separate focal networks shrink in size and their mutual networks grow.[69] This finding, if generalized to the organizational situation has important implications because, among other things, it reduces an individual's weak ties, with important consequence for the access of the two parties to a diverse array of information.[70]

Thus the nature of the larger organizational context interacts to determine the extent to which the parties are uniquely constrained by the actions of the other. The nature of multiplexity within a whole series of relationships determines the extent of impact. If they depend on each other exclusively for a wide variety of things, then supervisors and subordinates are heavily constrained by each other. But in the modern, more pluralistic organization, individuals can develop a patch work of uniplex relationships each of which provides a piece of their larger array of needs. In addition, individuals can seek out relationships with others outside the organization to compensate for bad organizational relationships.

Another important interacting factor in determining the impact of a superior on a subordinate is their respective positioning in networks of work relationships. In the case of SSCR perhaps the most well-known effect of individual positioning is the Pelz effect. An essential part of the supervisory function is to manage relationships between his/her unit and other entities within the organization.[71] The Pelz effect suggests that to have influence over subordinates, a supervisor must be perceived by them as having influence outside of the work unit.[72]

In the interpersonal communication literature there has been a growing recognition that our separate relationships are affected by the relationships we have with others.[73] Thus our dyadic relationships are seen as affected by their embeddedness in social contexts. The work of Parks and his colleagues has been particularly important in this regard.[74]

A major factor in the development of SSCR, then, is the chain of interdependent needs that they have with each other and with other people within and outside their work unit. Typically dyads such as the SSCR have been treated as individual units and their role in more general vertical communication has been ignored.[75] However, technological imperatives, especially those associated with role sender's needs, heavily influence the content of communication that flows within a role set.[76] These communications are one of the most direct indications of interdependencies and coordination requirements existing within an organization. In fact, as Katz and Kahn note, occupants of the offices to which roles are tied are usually associated with a limited number of others who are adjacent to them in the workflow structure or the hierarchy of authority of an organization (e.g., supervisors and subordinates).[77]

There are many elements of the larger organizational context, such as pay and promotion systems, which can impinge on an SSCR. One issue which is typically overlooked in the literature on SSCR is the general norm of behavior which exists within the organization toward particular types of relationships. The surrounding organization may "condition" the way in which the behavior of a supervisor affects subordinates.[78] On one level there may be specific expectations governing how to interact with a supervisor.[79] On another level there may be an experiential factor concerning individual perceptions and the history of interaction with others in the organization.

These contextual factors relating to the human environment of the SSCR provide a medium in which any particular relationship is played out. They provide a point of comparison to determine the evaluation of any one particular relationship and thus in many ways serve as a basis for interpreting the significance of relationships. Thus these factors constitute part of an interpretive framework for understanding individual relationships. Issues of proportion also provide individuals with a set of expectations of what is likely to occur in any prospective relationships. These expectations are likely to condition the responses of subordinates to superiors, at least initially.

The SSCR is very permeable, admitting many influences from the outside that constrain it and mediate its potential impacts providing a framework for assessing interactions, contraindications, and dysfunctions related to dosage. While undeniably it is the most important single dyadic relationship in an organization, it is enmeshed in a network of other, often redundant relationships, which offer both the individual and the organization multiple means of accomplishing their objectives.

Conclusion

The management of interpersonal relationships, particularly the SSCR, has a number of implications for the dosage metaphor:

- For relationships, in terms of frequency, sometimes one message is enough to permanently alter a relationship.
- Amount often determines the depth (e.g., social penetration) of a relationship, especially if the therapeutic agent involved passes thresholds in the sequencing of increasingly intimate, reciprocated disclosures.
- The notions of over and under benefiting and inequity driving relationships also suggest a degree of reciprocity and follow expectations in relationships driven by exchange dynamics.
- Interpersonal approaches are the most reductionist, most limited in what they have to say about delivery systems, presumably because of their focus on the "gold standard" of face-to-face interactions.
- Trust is a critical interaction factor in self-disclosures, and the social milieu one is in effects compliance gaining strategies. If subordinates have limited alternatives for relationships, then a supervisor can significantly impact their organizational experience.

- Clear contraindications exist: disclosure is limited if it is perceived that it could damage the relationship or that someone may reveal private information to others.
- The ideology of openness may have caused significant harm to relationships, representing a clear dysfunction of over dosage.

CHAPTER 5

Productivity

Improvements in worker effectiveness (as a substantial amount of organizational costs are associated with labor and are thereby linked to communication) offer much potential for improving productivity. However, "… the chain of conditions between amount of communication in the workplace and outcomes such as satisfaction, effectiveness, or other effects may be quite lengthy."[1]

We will use productivity in its broadest sense here, focusing on the generation of wealth in a variety of forms entailing social as well as economic capital, which also suggests some degree of efficiency and effectiveness. While on the surface it may appear that there is a clear link between communication and productivity, somewhat disconcertingly very little is known about this relationship.[2] "Productivity is simultaneously one of the most important and most difficult variables for communication researchers to study."[3]

Efficiency is fundamentally concerned with what level of input, particularly in terms of expending the least effort possible (i.e., the lowest dose) needed to achieve certain outputs. This precisely parallels fundamental approaches to dosage and the dose-response curve discussed earlier. *Efficiency* is obviously an important pragmatic issue because it allows:

- attention and effort to be more profitably devoted elsewhere;
- producing a desired effect for the minimum amount of effort, expense, or waste; or
- an attractive ratio of effective work outcomes to energy expended.

In this chapter I first turn to some empirical findings related to how a minimal amount of communication can still produce desired impacts.

In a transition section I specifically discuss the upper and lower bounds of communication activities in relationship to the classic concept of information load. In the next section I turn more explicitly to the ideas of match and associated cost–benefit equations. This chapter concludes with takeaways for extending the dosage metaphor to productivity.

Empirical Findings

My first research paper focused on the normative level of communication activities in a range of organizational content networks.[4] It demonstrated surprisingly low levels of communication in organizations. My current interest in dosage stems, in part, from my extensive, longitudinal research program focused on the Cancer Information Service Research Consortium (CISRC), a somewhat unique virtual organization comprised of researchers and practitioners.[5] The CISRC had levels of communication that did not conform to either our normative or theoretic understandings of innovation processes. They did, however, conform to other empirical findings.[6]

At the outset, following the diffusion of innovation literature, we focused on interpersonal communication in the CISRC. However, perhaps our most convincing over-time finding was the most disturbing one—the low and declining intervention strategy communication rates. This consistent empirical finding flies in the face of network models of the diffusion of innovations.[7] These models privilege direct, interpersonal, cohesive communication as the primary means by which influence related to adoption of particular innovations is diffused through a system by contagion processes which we will detail in the next chapter.

It has been my experience that when the CISRC network analysis findings are shared with others, the first reaction is to question the quality of the data. It was partly this sort of response from CIS staff that led to our switch midway through the project to include facsimile and electronic mail (e-mail) in the communication logs in an attempt to uncover additional communication related to innovation. In the end, the weight of the evidence was compelling; it may be time to look elsewhere for explanations, several of which we discuss below.

A Minimalist Perspective

Simply put, it could be the case that *not much communication is needed to achieve certain effects*. In spite of the concerns of persuasion scholars for overcoming resistance, and such shibboleths of communication theory as repetition is critical for getting a message across, in most organizations orders are orders. If my organization says that henceforward all of my communication related to invoices will be by e-mail, as long as the system is minimally intrusive, relatively easy to use, and not personally risky (or there are more risks for not going along), I do what is required of me. In most organizations this sort of compliance may not be difficult to achieve and the communication related to it may be minimal,[8] especially compared to the winning of hearts and minds assumed by most participation theories.[9]

It may be the case that for a number of innovations, minimalist communication strategies involving some mediated communication and intense interpersonal communication involving only those immediately affected may be the best approach. Dosage issues related to staging and the management of uncertainty determine how rich channels should be and how much information is necessary at different points, especially because acquiring more information can result in delays and increased costs.[10]

Structural Equivalence

Burt's[11] introduction of structural equivalence notions to innovation research was perhaps the first systematic attempt to offer an alternate explanation to the classic taken-for-granted assumptions relating to direct interpersonal communication in diffusion theory.[12] This approach argues that a person's position exposes them to information that influences their actions regardless of their direct, cohesive communication with others. In addition, competitive motivations may impel individuals to act to maintain or to gain particular advantages. From a structural equivalence perspective, it may be the case that no cohesive interpersonal communication is required to trigger the appropriate intervention strategy's implementation.

Tacit Understandings

Another way of approaching this problem is through an individual's understanding of the underlying rules of a game. When I am passed the ball in basketball, I may be well drilled in formalized approaches, and see a pattern that activates a play that is implicitly understood by all of the other players. Thus the high levels of formalization characteristic of the CISRC may have minimized the need for direct, interpersonal communication.[13] Alternatively I may go with the flow of events, reacting spontaneously, and experience the pleasurable sensation of jamming,[14] where others react in concert with me and our combined actions achieve our ultimate purpose of scoring a basket. In both of these situations, *direct overt communication is not needed; rather, tacit understandings of the rules of the game and what my actions entail within this established framework are what is required* to play.

In these situations the manager may act as a curious combination of coach and umpire, setting the overall rules framework and then making sure that they are followed. This approach also explains how people deal with so many competing task demands: in effect, some players let others carve out their own turf and delegate to them implicitly (or formally through task forces or Communities of Practice more informally) the accomplishment of particular tasks. (As long as they have the ball, let them run with it; when they pass it off, then we will see what I do.) So players do not become involved until they need to act. Given the preliminary research trials characteristic of the CISRC projects, members may not have felt a need to communicate until wide-scale implementation was likely. All parties were relatively busy, committed to different goals, and were in effect willing to have a "conspiracy of silence" as long as their tacit agreements were not broken. In this sense further communication would only make their everyday working lives worse.

Looking in the Wrong Place at the Wrong Time

As we have suggested, perhaps the most important communication occurred before the trials of the various interventions even began, in the initial buy-in phase of the CISRC. After this point, it was just a question of operationalizing original commitments, primarily through the training of information specialists, events that we did not specifically measure. Thus it could be the case that the original project ideas were explained so well and commitment was so total that there was not a need for a major ongoing communication effort. This has been termed as left-hand censoring; a failure to detect change because it happened before the first data collection.[15] Bach also has suggested that organizational members make their judgments on how to act toward an innovation in the seminal development phase—before it is introduced.[16] Essentially, after this point only a low level of maintenance, fine-tuning, would be needed for the ongoing operation of the project.

It could also be the case in the extremely rich, complex communication environment of the CISRC that we just did not focus on the critical communication events. Perhaps, in spite of our societal and academic privileging of interpersonal communication, this may not be the appropriate level of analysis; group communication, in the form of face-to-face national meetings may be the best predictor. It was at these meetings that CISRC members could get a feel for whether a critical mass of their fellows were committed to the projects. With a visible awareness of the actions of their "competitors," individual thresholds could be reached for their continued involvement in the projects.[17] *Ultimately, in spite of what are on the face of it very low doses of communication, at least on some levels, the CISRC was successful.*[18]

Load

What volume of communication do we need to achieve particular purpose?

> *Too many meetings* is a frequent complaint, but *never having any meetings* and particularly *never having any contact with the leader* follow closely behind, as does the problem of poorly organized meetings.[19]

On the receiver's side there has been a concern with impacts of communication overloads in part because they can have similar outcomes to overdoses. For the transfer of information to engineers, too much can be as harmful as too little,[20] with uncertainty resulting from both too little and too much information.[21] In the organizational design literature much attention has been devoted to issues of how we arrange organizational systems to control for overloads.[22] However, there has not been concomitant interest in underloads and the, perhaps, related topic of ignorance. This is one area where balance, matching of various factors to keep load within a certain range, is critical to individual and organizational performance.[23]

Integration, as Lawrence and Lorsch[24] also argued, can lead to "an indiscriminate increase in connectedness [that] can be a drag on productivity, as people get bogged down in maintaining all their relationships."[25] Dense communication within organizations has been found to be related to low production, low morale, and an experience of chaos.[26] There is a threshold "... beyond which market knowledge depth and cross-functional collaboration may have detrimental effects on performance."[27] A variety of treatments (or coping mechanisms) have been proposed for message overload, including specialization, sampling information, omission, priority systems, development of networks, and modification of messages (e.g., conciseness).[28] In part, because of individual and system overloads, organizations must achieve efficiencies in their internal communication systems by message routing and message summarizing[29] or condensing.[30]

Underload situations and organizational slack increase the opportunities individuals have for communication and, perhaps, innovation, but they may not be clearly related to organizational objectives. Underload, aside from being wasteful of organizational resources, can lead to boredom and the need to make up interesting stimuli (e.g., gossip). Ultimately, underloads mean that needed doses are not being taken for the benefit of the entire organization.

Efficiency

Because of its graphic portrayals and associated mathematical indices, perhaps the area of communication most suited for efficiency research is network analysis. (See the illustrative box on small group structure, Box 5.1.) Various approaches have been made to determining the efficiency of networks with most detailing a relationship between the number of communication links necessary to perform a particular task. For example, short-path links are better for obtaining knowledge than long ones; they are both more efficient because of fewer links and contain less possibility for distortion and error.[31] *Network analysis, through various linkage metrics, offers many precise and elegant ways (e.g., small world) of specifying the minimum number of communication linkages needed to contact others.* Efficient networks minimize the number of direct contacts with decision makers; however, it also appears that supervisors will only delegate when overloaded with information.[32] More formally, graph efficiency is the degree to which the number of links is the minimum necessary to prevent splintering the network into separate parts, the more efficient the more fragile the network, the more likely that some redundancy is needed for robustness, effectiveness.[33]

Box 5.1
Small Group Structure

Network analysis can be applied to problems relating to dosage and productivity in the context of classic findings relating to small groups and teams. We start with the initial conditions for most of these experiments with people in cubicles that have openings through which messages can be passed either open or shut depending on the type of structure being imposed on the group. This set of conditions provide a basic structure, much like an organizational chart does, and individuals do not have to use all of the opportunities available to them. Unlike the typical organization, however, in these experimental conditions individuals do not have the possibility to adjust their own dosages by creating informal linkages with others that go beyond those specified for them.

Connectivity and density are also critical indicators of groups propensity toward creativity and conformity with ties to diverse others needed for the latter and greater density of ties associated with the latter. Both of these indicators are associated with the amount or frequency of communication, or both, ties within a group.

(Continued)

(*Continued*)

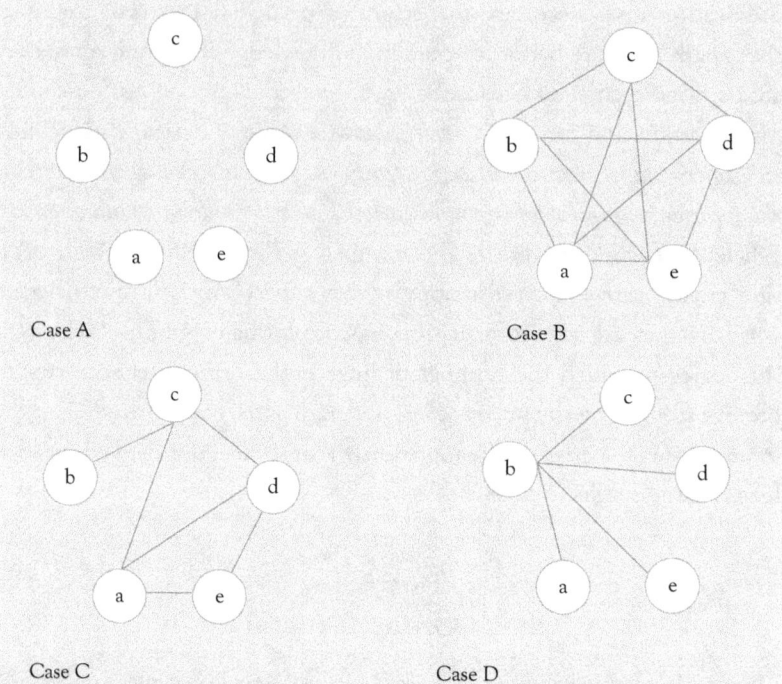

Figure 5.1. Communication networks, productivity, and dosage.

In Case A and Case B in Figure 5.1 we have the two extremes with no links in one and all of the possible communication links, in the case of a five-person network 20 (5 × 4) links, in the other. In Case B the network is totally decentralized and people are free to choose with whom they will communicate, but this freedom also can quickly lead to overloads, overdoses if all linkages are utilized. Inevitably, over time in Case B some structure arises in these networks to match the group effort to the task at hand. This might be represented by Case C where the group discovers that member C is a math whiz. All of the group members then transmits to C all the information they have related to a math problem, while A, D, and E exchange information on a crossword puzzle they are working on to pass the time until C solves the math problem, thus preventing some of the attendant problems with underload. The connectiveness score for this group is 0.7. Finally, in Case D, we have the classic highly centralized group, with a similar math problem, for which the experimenter has constrained the communication structure in such a way that only B has direct contact with all of the group members (a connectiveness score of 0.4). B is not a math whiz, so they relay all of the information to C and when C solves the problem, B must relay this solution back to A, D, and E. All of this relaying introduces the possibility of error and delay and attendant reductions in productivity.

In sum, communication structure as indicated by the connectiveness scores in social networks, has direct implications for how productive a group might be both in terms of efficiency (using the appropriate number of links to handle a problem) and in terms of the ultimate effectiveness of the group. Overdoses of linkages also create other potential problems such as excess conformity associated with greater cohesiveness.

There also has been some attention devoted to the strength of particular links. So weak ties may facilitate search, but impede transfer. However, strong ties are costly to maintain[34] and therefore should be used most for tacit knowledge and other difficult transfer problems. A study of an online graduate class's one-to-one postings on a class discussion board found that prestige and centrality were robust predictors of cognitive learning.[35] A recent meta-analysis suggests that teams with densely configured interpersonal ties, which result in more information sharing and collaboration, attain their goals better and are more committed to staying together, in spite of the observation that large numbers of direct ties are costly to maintain.[36]

Small Group Communication Networks

Perhaps more systematic research has been conducted on small group communication networks than any other area of research related to communication structures. The research results related to task performance and structure appear to fit quite nicely into a contingency theory framework and the idea of a match between structure and performance.

The experimental situation in small-group (typically five individuals) network studies was found to constrain the written messages that could flow between group members.[37] The primary distinction was between *centralized* communication networks, where some individuals were clearly the hub in communication flows and could, in effect, act as gatekeepers for other individuals, and *decentralized* structures in which there was more than one way of routing a message and no one individual dominated. Key players would be likely to be selected as leaders of centralized groups by other members. In addition, there was also clear evidence that central members were more satisfied than peripheral ones and that the overall level of satisfaction was higher in decentralized groups.[38]

Most of the research studies in this area focused on the performance of groups with different structures on simple and complex tasks. Shaw found clear evidence of a relationship between effectiveness in the performance of particular types of tasks and the relative degree of centralization of these groups. For simple problems, such as symbol identification, the centralized groups were more efficient in terms of time, sent fewer messages, and made fewer errors. For complex problems, such as sentence construction, decentralized groups took less time and made fewer errors, but they still sent more communication messages.[39]

Shaw adopted the concept of *saturation* to explain these findings. For complex problems the most central person quickly becomes overloaded with both information and the burden of relaying information to other group members. When the group is faced with a simple task the volume of communication can be easily handled and there is a benefit to having a central repository of information. However, the independence possible in decentralized groups permits the sharing of the relaying burden of information among group members and it also results in a better "match" of individual capabilities to the problems confronting the group.

Guetskow and Simon, in an interesting twist on prior experiments, speculated that one of the reasons centralized groups were more efficient was that they had, in effect, been provided with a plan of action for making decisions.[40] They discovered that if decentralized groups had an opportunity to discuss group organization after they had some experience with the task they became just as efficient as more centralized groups in performing simple tasks. Decentralized groups became more efficient by reducing the number of linkages that were used within the group. Other research studies have also suggested that there is a general *trend overtime for efficient groups to reduce the number of communication linkages used*, to in effect become more structured, or to match their structure to the task at hand.[41] Indeed, some have argued that these processes can be generalized to a broad range of systems; that because of their *efficiencies highly structured hierarchies are inevitable*.[42]

Cost/Benefit Analyses

The costs of information acquisition are many: psychological, temporal, and material.

> As the number of direct ties increases, network costs may outweigh the benefits derived from network resources, turning social capital into social liability. As the size of the network grows, adding network partners may result in diminishing returns or even negative effects.[43]

They are also impacted by the nature of communication structures.

> If benefits of identity are to lower the costs of communication and coordination, they come at a cost. For identities represent a norm which indicates avenues of exploration: by implication, they also prohibit certain paths.[44]

Information seeking has been one area of communication research that has traditionally examined issues of effort and the avoidance of information. Most seekers appear to assume it is better to rely on easily obtained information, they have an answer after all, no matter how dubious, than to spend the effort necessary to get complete information. The "costs" are real in terms of extra time and effort for a complete information search, which also may result in delayed opportunities, complicated decision-making, and increased information overload. There are also additional psychological costs, such as the loss of self-esteem and frustration that result from an unsuccessful search.

The classic *law of "least effort"* has been evoked to articulate why channels are chosen first that involve minimal exertion. The earliest expression of this was *Zipf's law*,[45] a more general expression of a wide range of human behavior, which suggests that seekers will minimize their efforts, even when it means accepting lower quality content.[46] A corollary of this law is that people will tend to return to sources they used in the past. Needless to say, this suggests the sort of localized, relatively sparse communication structures actually observed in the empirical studies of the CISRC presented at the beginning of this chapter.

In many ways the research related to the importance of access are some of the most compelling in the social science literature. A consistent set of findings suggest that the threshold point where a source is considered inaccessible is very low. For example, people will not invest much of their time to learn internet search engines and typically rely on a very limited number of commands.[47]

Even more disturbing is that access also may be the single most important criterion in evaluation by users of an information system.[48] So *accessibility outweighs quality in determining usage of information* from particular sources. In fact, it is a common finding that individuals will knowingly rely on inferior information sources for answers to their problems, because it would take too much effort to get authoritative information.[49] A number of studies document cases in which organizational members seek out information from inferior sources because of the reduced costs involved.[50] Allen, in his research stream involving communication in research and development laboratories, consistently found that professionals will seek the most readily accessible source of information, both in terms of physical distance and comprehensibility, rather than the "best" sources, which offer more professionally authoritative information.[51]

Search problems are often related to the "costs" of information seeking compared to the value or benefit of the information sought, particularly in relation to decision-making.[52] One of the more troubling issues in information seeking is the lack of persistence of information seekers and related issues of accessibility. In short, people do not typically put forward much effort in information seeking and can easily be deterred by obstacles.[53]

More recent work in this area has focused on *information foraging*,[54] a form of cost/benefit analysis which assumes that humans maximize gains of valuable information per unit cost. Resource costs are the expenditures of time and energy involved in obtaining information. Opportunity costs represent what could have been gained by pursuing other activities. Accordingly, seekers minimize access costs by putting information resources close to them; they reduce costs of getting from one patch of information to another; they look for patches that are exceptionally rich in their yield; and they maximize nutritional return in their diet, avoiding "junk food," being cognizant of energy returned versus handling time. A key issue for this approach is the notion of "picking up scents" that lead to valuable patches containing the dosage individuals seek.

Managing Attention and Satisficing

The most basic limit for most of us is time. "... acquisition of information is costly. At the minimum, it requires attention, which is always in scarce supply ..."[55] Even for the most trivial tasks, information seeking could theoretically consume a lifetime, if all the information needed to understand them was gathered. The problem then is not in deciding to seek information, but in deciding when to stop. Adept decision makers know intuitively when they have gathered enough information for any particular purpose. They satisfice. They develop their own intuition on when they have spent as much energy as they can in deciding what they should do about any particular problem that confronts them and searching for information related to it. They also learn to approximate, or to reach a judgment on when they can make a high enough quality decision for any particular event.[56] Thus, decision makers search for an appropriate solution, not *the* optimal solution. They reach these judgments because they have developed an appreciation for what their limits are; they can mentally weigh only so much information at any given time. Examining issues relating to satisficing and access introduce us to the seeming irrationality of people who grapple with information, communication, and uncertainty daily in their lives. The ultimate goals of rationality, may be to develop a sense of coherence, and a simple one at that, with satisficing the standard rather than maximizing.[57]

Conclusion

Our comfortable shibboleths do not stand up to close empirical scrutiny. Most communication theories assume that more communication is better and imply high volumes are beneficial, but the few studies that have been done suggest, at best, complex contingencies and cost/benefit equations that directly relate to the following takeaways related to dosage.[58]

- Productivity is summed up brilliantly by the dose–response curve, at least for efficiency.
- When considering amount and frequency, managers would be best served by starting with the most minimal dose possible which points to a fundamental rule of sequencing as well, starting with the lowest possible dose before proceeding to stronger ones.
- As Daft and Lengel pointed out, delivery systems should be matched to the task at hand. Reaching out and touching someone with direct interpersonal contact is very expensive and should only be done as a last resort.[59]
- Interactions: Resource scarcity and abundance may be equally problematic, tempting one to do too little and too much, respectively.
- Contraindications: Too much communication often leads to confusion and delays.

In sum, too much communication quickly can lead to dysfunctional consequences and actually result in worsening the problems it is intended to solve.

CHAPTER 6

Change

The dosage metaphor is probably most amenable to problems of change, which inevitably ask what is it we need to do to cause a particular reaction in an individual or a social system? But, "... metaphors should not be seen as a means for sugar coating bitter pills."[1] We will examine the implementation of innovations in one organizational setting before turning to the broader problem of transfer both within and between organizations. Following Everett Rogers' approach to the diffusion of innovations we explicitly incorporate interpersonal and mass communication, in part, by applying network analysis to this problem.[2]

Implementation

Successful implementation of an innovation, once it is transferred, can be conceived of as the *routinization, incorporation, and stabilization* into the ongoing work activity of an organizational unit. For organizations, "the bottom line is implementation (including its institutionalization), and not just the adoption decision."[3]

Advocating change necessarily results in increasing *uncertainty*, which can lead to resistance to innovation by adoption units. Communication plays a key role in overcoming resistance in part by reducing uncertainty. Complexity and risk are elements of uncertainty which are crucial to the ultimate implementation of innovations. *Complexity* relates to the number of potential alternatives perceived in an innovation's adoption. *Risk* is the perceived consequences to the adoption unit associated with the implementation of an innovation. Overcoming perceptions of risk and complexity is crucial to inducing the level of involvement needed,[4] because cooperative norms are often essential to the implementation of innovations.[5]

The reduction of uncertainty inherent in communication can decrease resistance to innovations, but usually decision units also must exert some degree of power and influence to facilitate implementation. In fact, the communication channels available to transmit the various types of power and information concerning innovations are the primary structural characteristics which affect innovation implementation. The commonly used types of power in organizational settings have different communication costs associated with them and they also result in different levels of involvement in adoption units. These *communication costs* are determined by the amount of resources expended in the transmission of a message,[6] a rather direct manifestation of dosage. Some combinations of power, complexity, and risk can overload available channels (or delivery systems), creating an upper limit to the capacity of an organization to implement certain innovations.[7] In more decentralized environments, messages from a wide range of sources may actually be more effective and less costly for an organization than exclusively relying on a top–down approach to innovation.[8] The complexity and perceived risk inherent in innovations interact with types of power to determine the communication costs associated with their implementation. This introduces notions of the interaction of a number of therapeutic agents to produce desired impacts.

Fidler and Johnson described the consequences of using various types of influence processes in innovation implementation.[9] Using the classic framework of French and Raven,[10] the relatively high communication costs of the use of sanction and persuasion are contrasted by the low costs of using legitimate and referent power. They also contrasted the higher levels of involvement induced by classic influence types of power represented by persuasion, expert, and referent power, with the lower levels of involvement resulting from sanction and legitimate power. Expert power represents some special problems for the person exercising it. If every step leading to a judgment must be explained to the other party, especially in situations of high tacit knowledge, then very high communication costs may be involved. On the other hand, if just a summative answer is needed, then its costs may be as low as those of legitimate power. Paradoxically the more an expert needs to explain, the less power he may ultimately have because he is transferring his basis of influence to the other person.

Complexity also affects the types of power that will be used to promote innovation implementation and those that might be contraindicated. For example, the more facets to an innovation, the more actions that have to be rewarded and somewhat relatedly, the greater the volume of information related to persuasion. Thus the high communication costs of persuasion and sanction (and also, in this case, expert power) increase almost exponentially with greater complexity; however, the communication costs of other types of power increase more linearly because the invocation of these types of power is inherent in the messages concerning innovation.

Generally, persuasive strategies have been found to be the most effective means of ensuring the successful implementation of innovations, especially highly risky and complex ones. Effective persuasion can best overcome resistance attributable both to lack of understanding and to fear; in addition, the use of persuasion results in a higher level of involvement. Indeed, the path between uncertainty and willingness to participate showed only a moderate, negative relationship in one study,[11] which confirms the view that firms must build in an ethos of risk taking, a system of rewards for accepting and adapting to change, for innovation to prosper.[12]

For informal channels *persuasion*, or influence, is the primary means available to secure participation in an innovation. Persuasion rests on the capacity of an individual to cause changes in another's behavior by the use of more subtle, informal, and often cognitively oriented means than those associated with sanction or authority.[13] In utilizing persuasion, an individual communicates evidence, arguments, and a rationale advocating acceptance of an innovative idea and participation in an innovation, with organizational efforts very similar to the campaigns discussed later in this chapter. Because innovations within large organizations generally are initiated by an idea generator who must convince others to participate,[14] the willingness to participate in innovations is a critical outcome of communication. As effective persuasion results in greater participation in the implementation of innovations, it usually entails less resistance to the eventual implementation of innovations as well, and it is more likely to insure active involvement. There is a critical difference between effective communication, where each party understands the other, and persuasive communication, where one of them changes their opinion as a result of communication.[15]

Transfer of Knowledge

Diffusion, and relatedly the transfer of innovative ideas, has been very problematic across and within organizations. Perhaps no area in the organizational literature has depended more on metaphor than that focusing on organizational change and innovation, with organizations viewed as learning systems;[16] the presence of hooks, things in one's own experience that they can attach new knowledge to in Leonard's[17] terms, or *stickiness* in Szulanski's,[18] evoking images of immobility, inertness, and inimitability. So in a way we have a replication in broad form of Berlo's[19] classic *Source–Message–Channel–Receiver* or SMCR (See illustrative Box 6.1) model with stickiness a characteristic of sources, messages and channels the province of knowledge brokers, and absorptive capacity a property of receivers.

Box 6.1
This Is Harder Than It Looks

Rational explication of communication and innovation processes often leaves the impression that convincing someone to adopt an innovation should be a rather simple, straightforward process. This is especially so because of the pervasive application of the container/conduit metaphors of communication and of the widely recognized pro-innovation bias in US culture with an assumption that innovation and change are inherent goods and communication is a simple matter of transferring messages. But over the years, the recognition that the overwhelming majority of innovations fail forces one to confront the hard reality that transfer, adoption, and implementation of innovation is much harder than it looks. At times the needed dose for highly complex innovations that require persuasion may exceed an organization's structural capacity to communicate.

A classic communication model that can be used to explicate this problem is the one developed by David Berlo at Michigan State University in the early 1960s. The SMCR model detailed the characteristics of each component of the model. Both the source and receiver have certain communication skills, attitudes, and knowledge. They are also members of particular social systems and cultures. The more similarities they share across these characteristics, the more homophilous they are and the more likely it is that communication will be successful. Messages can vary in their content, elements, treatment, structure, and the codes used to express them. Channels, in the original formulation, focused on our classic five senses, hearing, seeing, touching, smelling, and tasting, but have since expanded to include other means of message transmission including various media (which inherently contain a cluster of senses they activate). Later, because of a realization that messages were not easily transferred, that meanings were lodged in the people that interpreted them and not inherent properties of the messages themselves, the importance of feedback was also recognized. A responsible communicator should not assume that just because a message is delivered it would provoke the desired reaction. He needed some sort of affirmative response that the original meaning had been invoked in the receiver.

The source in this framework needed to encode a message in such a way that they were likely to be successful. This encoding often has direct relationships to the dosage metaphor because a source needs to assess the number and kinds of messages needed to provoke the desired reaction. But over the years the recognition of the role of tacit knowledge has grown along with the introduction of the concept of stickiness. Some ideas, processes, and practices just do not transfer well from individuals or from particular social settings. It may, indeed, be very hard to communicate certain innovations. This is further exacerbated by the reluctance of many people to voice certain ideas because of social norms or concerns with face in certain cultures.

Of course messages themselves can also be problematic. They are often laden with jargon (itself in a way a form of tacit knowledge) and complex. The more complex they are the more difficult it is going to be to successfully transfer them. One characteristic of the modern world is the increasing availability of information and with it a dazzling

(Continued)

(*Continued*)

(and often bewildering) array of choices and attendant uncertainty in weighing the alternatives associated with them.

Recognition of equivocality of messages then led, as we have seen in the chapter devoted to match, to the realization in media richness theory that one had to choose channels that matched the difficulty of the problems one was confronting. So it is widely held that interpersonal channels are more effective for persuasion because of the wide range of senses that can be used in face-to-face communication, activating an array of potential delivery systems for any dose one might want to deliver.

Receivers, finally, must decode messages that the source has encoded. They may not have the requisite absorptive capacity to understand a message because of lack of time, resources, skills, or knowledge. Further, some ideas may just not be particularly good ones. So it is increasingly recognized that resistance may not be based on stubbornness, ignorance, or lassitude, but may occur because the receiver has a tacit understanding that certain ideas will just not work in particular contexts.

The recognition of all these problems and the high failure rate of innovations in actual practice have led to a change of emphasis in the innovation literature from its early presumption that adoption was the hard part, to a growing recognition that adoption is merely the beginning of the process; often even more attention needs to be devoted to implementation.

Stickiness research seeks to address a common managerial frustration, the failure of best practices to spread within organizations. One study found that only 13 percent of managers thought their firm was doing a good job of transferring knowledge internally, partly because of internal competitive forces.[20] Szulanski also discusses retentive capacity or the ability of a recipient to institutionalize and utilize new knowledge as an important factor. How sticky knowledge is is determined by its breadth, depth, specificity, and tacitness,[21] all related to dosage conceptions.

Absorptive capacity reflects the ability to recognize the value of new information, assimilate it, and apply it.[22] It is not enough to merely be exposed to knowledge, one must be able to internalize it, something that directly relates to the dosage metaphor, as well as to absorptive capacity. Absorptive capacity is not just about what is given, but the amount that any entity can actually absorb or receive. "Human communication will almost always go astray unless real energy is expended."[23]

In their original research Cohen and Levinthal sought to explain,[24] from an economic perspective, how R&D laboratories not only generate new knowledge, but also increase a firm's capacity to identify, assimilate, and exploit existing information, as well as predict with greater accuracy the nature of future technological advances. In other words a firm must invest for the long term in resources that enable it to assimilate new information by expanding its knowledge base so that it can more readily absorb all sorts of information and translate it into actionable knowledge useful for commercial purposes. Several factors can increase the potential for units to have high absorptive capacity, cross-functional interfaces, participation in decision-making, and job rotation, while others (e.g., elements of socialization processes) relate to a unit's realized capacity.[25] However, reverse engineering or mere observation of creative, innovative products may not fully capture the underlying tacit knowledge that goes into their production.[26] Absorptive capacity has been extended to represent all of a firm's dynamic capabilities for knowledge creation and utilization.[27]

Paradoxically the more people communicate, the more they converge on a common attitude, the less creative (different) the organization is. However, while cohesion limits creativity, it aids the spread and transfer of knowledge. The key problem, then, for managers is to find a balance among these paradoxical forces. Interestingly March demonstrated that in closed systems, as organizations became more knowledgeable and eliminated differences in understanding codes, they converged on equilibrium beliefs (that may or may not be accurate).[28] Higher learning rates, somewhat disconcertingly, lead to achieving this equilibrium earlier. They also can produce *competency traps* where, because of initial success, teams quickly converge on limited courses of action and are unwilling to consider new approaches.[29]

"Slow learning on the part of individuals maintains diversity longer, thereby providing the exploration that allows the knowledge found in organizational codes to improve."[30] This slow learning is facilitated by heterogeneity and greater specialization and the high communication costs associated with truly sharing diverse perspectives in groups.[31] Similarly, in a turbulent environment, a moderate level of turnover, coupled with slow socialization (which permits an opportunity for the organization to learn from individuals) slows the development of an equilibrium that is not an adaptive one. All of this suggests the delicate, temporal challenges (and the sequencing of doses) for organizations which wish to maintain diversity and the importance of processes that lead to uniformity of attitudes and behaviors and higher productivity.[32]

There may be an underlying nonlinear, inverted U-shaped element to these processes, as we discussed in Chapter 2, with some contact (often through small-world processes) necessary for stimulation, but too much contact resulting in conformity pressures,[33] although work still needs to be done on the contingencies involved for varying industries.[34] Or, stated in a different way, local search and reuse of existing knowledge results in rigidity, while expanding the scope of the search introduces the new, but may also introduce unreliability in organizational outputs.[35]

Strength of Weak Ties

The strength of weak ties has been intimately tied to the flow of information, and the transfer of knowledge, as we saw in Chapter 4, by definition is removed from stronger social bonds, such as influence and multiplex relations. Strong contacts are likely to be people with whom there is a constant sharing of the same information, and as a result individuals within these groupings have come to have the same information base. However, information from outside this base gives unique perspectives and, in some instances, strategic advantages over competitors in a person's immediate network, somewhat evocative of the exploration–exploitation findings we just discussed.

All of this again suggests the nature of match, the importance of measured dosages. While strong direct ties have compelling advantages for influence, the transfer of tacit knowledge, and potential spillover effects for resource sharing, they are costly to maintain and redundant, especially so for the opportunity costs of reducing the number of weak ties we might have. On the other hand, indirect ties allow us to experiment and scan our environment widely for information, but they have difficulty transferring that knowledge—the classic search transfer problem identified by Hansen.[36] There also may be interaction, and potential substitution effects between these types of ties, with interesting questions concerning whether, for example, the transfer of explicit codified knowledge entails that many indirect ties (which are easier to maintain) may be more beneficial than a few intensive direct ties.[37] Similarly, uniplexity, or a narrow focus, facilitates information sharing by making it more likely a common perspective will develop.[38] Social contexts of relatively dense ties with redundant others can inhibit creativity, but they also build trust and cooperation while aiding the tacit transfer of knowledge and influence attempts related to innovation implementation.

Disconcertingly the very factors that promote creativity initially may lead to diminished performance as time goes on. So a number of factors inherent in diverse groups also serve as barriers to their developing creative products. For example, the lack of a common language/vocabulary often impedes creative performance.[39] Lack of perceived similarity in turn is a major stumbling block for the exchange of information between diverse parties essential to creativity.[40] In addition, group size is inevitably associated with the development of coalitions. Moreover, the breaking up of a group into subgroups/coalitions, has been found to diminish its creativity, in part because it limits the sharing of diverse perspectives.[41] Increased communication, in part, because it results in the development of common perspectives, and tenure, which, in addition to resulting in common perspectives, increases the likelihood of centralization and subgroup formation, have been found to decrease creativity in teams.[42] There may be a rather natural process in large organizations, with the first increments of constraint more deleterious to creativity than any subsequent ones.[43] It has been found that a combination of high internal centrality, which may constrain freedom of action, and a large number of external ties, which may be related to larger institutional conformity pressures, may not be the most conducive arrangement for creativity.[44]

Similarly, it has been suggested that small-world networks and performance for theatrical productions followed an inverted U-shaped function with the sharing of common rather than novel information when cohesiveness becomes too high and a more pronounced negative for low connectivity and cohesiveness is obtained.[45]

Social Contagion

The contrast between *cohesion* and *structural equivalence* views of social contagion is an important theoretic frame for the understanding of dosage impacts in communication networks and extending work on weak ties. *A major debate has developed within the social network literature about whether direct communication or forces related to competition are the major motive forces within social systems.* Burt[46] has argued that one motive force is the presence of competitors who occupy structurally similar positions. In contrast, a cohesion perspective, perhaps best represented in the work of Rogers and his colleagues[47] related to innovation, and the campaign literature we will discuss later in the next chapter, would suggest that direct communication results in changes in individuals.

Cohesion perspectives essentially argue that communication contacts determine the development of norms. Thus, cohesion focuses on the socializing effect of discussions. The central assumption of the cohesion perspective is that the more frequent and empathetic the communication between individuals is, the more likely their opinions and behaviors will resemble each other's.[48] Structural equivalence focuses on competition. In this view, supervisors could be expected to hold views similar to other supervisors because of their potential competitive roles in the network. This position requires that they maintain certain attitudes and behaviors. Thus, individuals may be the focus of similar information, requests, and demands from members of their role set, creating *an information field* which, when internalized, creates even more powerful pressures to conform than direct discussions with others.

Social contagion suggests that an individual reaches evaluations about ambiguous objects through a social process in which the evaluations of all the proximate others in the system are weighed. As a result, people who are proximate to each other (in terms of their communication linkages) in the social structure tend to develop "consensual standards" toward ambiguous objects.[49] When different individuals come to the same conclusions independently as a result of these processes this may be a key explanation of receptivity to tipping points. What one person says or does is contagious for other people within the same group. Thus, this theory suggests that ambiguous objects stimulate the contagion process which in turn leads to a social norm regarding a particular practice. However, the contagion process, the social mechanism, can operate in two conceptually related yet distinctive ways: cohesion and structural equivalence.

The first proximate mechanism that brings homogeneity is cohesion.[50] The cohesion model has a long history of being used as a predictor of attitudes and beliefs in the social sciences. The model posits that homophily between ego (the focal individual, the object of influence) and the alter (others in a network who may influence the ego) can be predicted by the strength of their intense and mutual relations with one another. "By communicating their uncertainties to one another regarding some empirically ambiguous object, people socialize one another so as to arrive at a consensual evaluation of the object."[51] Thus, the more frequent and empathic the bond is between ego and alter, the more likely they come to share attitudinal and behavioral tendencies. As summarized in Hartman and Johnson, "The ego is able to come to a normative understanding of the costs and benefits of specific actions and opinions in terms of the people with whom the discussions are held and thus reduce the ego's level of uncertainty."[52] Where cohesion concerns influential relations among individuals within a primary group, structural equivalence concerns relational patterns among individuals who occupy particular positions.[53]

Change is often assumed to be an ideational process implicating awareness, attitudes, and beliefs. As a result, social influence is critical to understanding the underlying dynamics and mechanisms of change.[54] It has become apparent that media effects are moderated by the social context of individuals. In addition, over the last several years a major debate has developed about whether direct communication or forces related to competition are the major motive forces for innovation adoption, a traditional focus of campaigns.[55] If competitors adopt an innovation and it is successful, this would put another individual at a competitive disadvantage. Thus the other has a structural interest in adopting innovations.

This entails an individual will adopt an innovation when a structurally similar alter does even if they are not in direct communication contact, a key perspective in a minimalist approach to dosage issues. From this theoretical framework, members of systems may adopt and implement innovations because they perceive there is a competitive advantage vis-à-vis others in doing so. An interesting twist to these arguments is that a prominent person may be even more compelled to adopt normative innovations because he wants to remain prominent.[56]

In contrast, a cohesion perspective is implicit in most communication approaches to change, suggesting that direct communication results in changes in the individual that result in the adoption of innovations. Thus enthusiastic supporters of an innovation may directly communicate with members who were not involved in its development. This enthusiasm is contagious and the members decide to adopt the innovation because of the credibility and persuasiveness of their colleagues.

In sum, both cohesion and structural equivalence approaches to social contagion have been linked to innovation adoption, with the former the traditional approach and the latter offering important new insights. More recently it has been argued that they can have complementary effects on knowledge transfer, with cohesion easing it by reducing competitive impediments and tie strength impacting the transfer of tacit knowledge.[57] Subsequent analysis of the classic Coleman, Katz, and Menzel[58] tetracycline study, a primary early source of support for cohesion perspectives, suggests that marketing efforts by drug companies were the primary sources of influence and cohesion actually had very little impact,[59] reinforcing the importance of mass media as well as interpersonal influence.[60] This suggests that someone's information fields and (in a more encompassing sense) their structurally equivalent positions within networks may be the primary determinants of the diffusion of innovations.

The formation of attitudes, and related cohesion processes, in human communication networks has long been a crucial concern in the social sciences generally. Indeed, there have been a number of mathematical models which in essence argue, from a cohesion perspective, that greater amounts (or doses) of communication result in greater attitude similarities within networks. Something more recently applied to noncontroversial change efforts in exchange networks that focus on fostering trust associated with friendships and shared identities across the entire organization, preventing the often natural withdrawal of organizational members into the self-interest of their cohesive groups.[61]

Traditional *discrepancy models* of attitude change have received empirical support in a number of contexts, and essentially hypothesize that attitude change is a function of the distance between initial attitudes and the rate of contact between any two communicators, a more formal expression of cohesion arguments.[62] Later approaches to formalizing public opinion change into equations, such as Fan's ideodynamic time trend theory, which was an attempt to correlate particular types of mass media exposure (e.g., a newspaper story on cocaine usage) with campaign effects.[63]

Similarly, especially for noncontroversial change, the key structural issue is how to strategically promote the widespread, rapid communication of the underlying notions using structural leverage.[64] Interestingly, McGrath and Krackhardt also argue that for controversial changes, to reduce the probability of backlash and resulting counterinfluence attempts, it is better to let change unfold, demonstrating its effectiveness, by piloting it at the periphery, before attempting widespread change.[65]

Discrepancy approaches support the notion that if an individual communicates intensively within a group, then over time she will converge on the group's consensus. However, if the individual has ties outside of the group then her attitude will be some linear combination of the proportion of time she spends communicating with others and the nature of their disparate attitude positions. Danowski found some support for these notions in studies of groups within a large eastern financial institution, although the relationships between group connectivity and member attitude uniformity were somewhat counterintuitive and more complex than expected.[66] One major limiting condition to these processes is the amount of information that an individual already possesses relating to a particular attitude. Woelfel and colleagues argue that the greater the amount of information which has been previously communicated to an individual, the lesser the likelihood that future messages can induce attitude change.[67] This finding is also supported in a meta-analysis of US health communication campaigns, which stresses the importance for achieving pronounced campaign effects for presenting new information.[68]

Huckfeldt, Johnson, and Sprague, while recognizing the inertial, autoregressive force of an individual's existing information base, also suggest that an individual's positioning in low density networks with ties to others who share their opinions will slow social change and the convergence on similar attitudes.[69]

In organizations, partially because of their differentiation into functional groupings, individuals within disparate groups will come to adopt unique perspectives often associated with their functions[70] and their professions. It might be expected that if there were enough ties present between groups, then a whole organization network would eventually come to reflect a common position on a particular attitude.[71] The underlying assumptions of this particular perspective have been empirically supported in the work of Albrecht who found that key communicators were more likely to be cognitively and attitudinally integrated into their organizations.[72] However, recognizing the openness of organizations to communication from other organizations, other institutions within the society (e.g., professional associations), and the mass media, it is unlikely that any organization will be isolated enough or long enough lived for the entities within them to come to convergence.

Similar arguments can also be advanced in the field of organizational culture. Erickson, while developing arguments from a different conceptual base, especially those related to structural equivalence and related processes of social comparison, has suggested a somewhat similar notion can be found in the development of belief systems of individuals in networks. A belief system is an organized diversity of attitudes that can be directly related to notions underlying organizational cultures.[73] Erickson contends that too many ties between groups will result in a commonality of positions, but she offers an interesting twist to the previous arguments. She contends that a moderate amount of ties between divergent groups is likely to result in stronger opposing belief systems, because these groups can now define themselves more clearly in their opposition to other groups.

More recently, work in this general area has focused on semantic networks[74] and, most evocatively, in the work on *Centering Resonance Analysis* (CRA), drawing on theoretical developments in social cognitive theory.[75] This approach focuses on identifying discursively important words and then representing them as a network.

At its heart, CRA focuses on the issue of resonance represented by the common occurrence of words in structurally similar positions in text. Kuhn and Corman's work focusing on planned change rests on the assumption "… that members' interpretations become *homogeneous* overtime, due to the social influence carried by communication practices."[76] Bridging cognition and action makes social cognitive approaches appealing. "Examining schemata can show how knowledge is dispersed among actors, as well as how collective knowledge works its way into the construction and reconstruction of their conceptual systems through participation in joint activity …"[77]

In the structural equivalence model, the driving force for similarity in perceptions is competition between ego and alter. The more the alter is able to substitute for the ego in the ego's role relations, the more pressure the ego feels to conform to the alter's attitudes or behaviors. "The ego comes to a normative understanding of the costs and benefits of the alter filling his or her role and a social understanding that is shared by others in similar roles."[78] From a structural equivalence perspective, direct communication contacts between individuals are not necessary for the development of a shared frame of reference.[79] Hartman and Johnson further explained that structurally equivalent individuals may experience more pressure toward uniformity because they "may be the focus of similar information, requests, and demands from members of their role set, creating an information field in which they are embedded, which, when internalized, creates even more powerful pressures to conform than discussions with similar alters."[80]

In sum, both cohesion and structural equivalence approaches to social contagion have been linked to the transfer of knowledge. *Cohesion perspectives fit clearly into the ideology of the communication metamyth that more is necessarily better, while structural equivalence perspectives relate more directly to minimalist views.*

Critical Mass and Threshold

As we have seen, network analysis is a key source of concepts that enrich our understanding of dosage within communication research. This is particularly so for diffusion of innovations. An important general property of a network link is its strength. Typically the frequency of communication is used to indicate the strength of a link; however, there are many possible indicants of the strength, each of which has different implications. For example, wide-ranging contacts of short duration may indicate individuals are searching for potential sources, while a few focused contacts of long duration may indicate the development of tacit meanings.

Another way of characterizing network relationships, one that allows complex simulations of the spread of information and the development of social systems, is in terms of a few simple interaction rules that govern their development into self-organizing systems. So the susceptibility of a node to infection (usually a disease, but sometimes a new idea) spread through direct contact with others represented by *threshold rules* and how connected the system is (strong cliques inoculate against the spread of new ideas) can determine the extent of *information cascades*.[81]

Valente in his systematic review of the diffusion of innovations literature adds threshold and critical mass as central generating mechanisms to diffusion processes.[82] He sought to explain the classic S-curve finding that after a slow building of early adopters, innovations take off suddenly. Threshold models of collective behavior suggest that individuals engage in behaviors when a sufficient proportion of others do, with varying individual thresholds. These variations account for the classic distributions of different innovation roles from early to late adopter in classic *S-curve* formulations.

These thresholds also play a critical role in information cascades, in effect *tipping points*, that cause widespread changes in social systems. It appears that the more heterogenous a network is, the greater the unique information in each link, the more susceptible it is to cascades.[83] Individuals in structural positions that expose them to more information earlier are more likely to be earlier adopters.[84]

These two variables can interact with each other, because once an individual adopts an innovation it lowers the thresholds of others because of decreased risk. The more individuals who adopt, the lower the levels of risk, setting in motion a snowball effect.[85] In general, informal coalition building is critical to the development of innovation processes,[86] if for no other reason than because some innovations, such as electronic messaging, need a substantial number of adopters for successful implementation.[87]

Critical mass represents the number of individuals needed before an innovation can spread to others. *A key problem for the diffusion of communication technologies is that a certain number of users are required to make them useful, a key factor in the diffusion of social networking sites.*

Summary

As Table 6.1 details, transfer approaches to change relate very richly to the dosage metaphor. *Amount* is a critical ingredient of most network analysis approaches, with one of its central concept the strength of weak ties referring directly to this element. It details the counterintuitive finding that innovations are more likely to flow from those people with whom we have little contact. Conversely cohesion approaches to contagion argue that significant amounts of communication are needed for transfer, which is somewhat in line with the issues of tacit versus explicit communication.

Table 6.1. Comparing Transfer Approaches and the Dosage Metaphor

Dosage elements	Transfer approach			
	Absorptive capacity	Strength of weak ties	Contagion	Threshold/ critical mass
Amount	Depends on size of R&D	Minimal	Depends on discrepancy	Critical levels
Frequency	Depends on investment	Infrequent	Low for structural equivalence	Critical levels
Sequencing	Outside-in	Strong follow-up	Repetition for cohesion	Staging
Delivery systems	Fields	Links	Links for cohesion	Links
Interactions	Environmental turbulence	Density, embeddedness	Information fields, existing information	Heterogeneity
Contraindications	Stability	Motivation, access	Resistance, density	Risk
Dysfunctions	High costs	Conformity	Lack of control, creativity	Innovation failure

Amount also becomes a critical issue for threshold and critical mass approaches with amounts determining whether or not the dynamics involved in these perspectives are activated. Absorptive capacity details that the size of an organization's R&D operations determines whether or not it can process the information needed to truly transfer new ideas from its environment, a critical issue we will return to in the next chapter.

As is the case with most of the theoretical approaches we have discussed, *frequency* is somewhat less clearly specified. For absorptive capacity, the frequency of communication with the external world depends on the organization's investment in R&D resources. Strength of weak ties entails infrequent communication with the other, with links that can decay very rapidly.[88] One of the unique aspects of dosage-related approaches from a structural equivalence perspective is that no direct communication with the other may be necessary for particular impacts. Frequency may have to build for the level needed to achieve certain thresholds.

Sequencing is an issue that is more implicitly covered than explicitly argued in these approaches. For absorptive capacity the presumption is that information is processed and brought into the organization, activated if you will, by R&D laboratories, who then act on the information internally. For weak-ties approaches there often is a presumption that once information is accumulated from weak ties, it then must be dealt with in terms of one's strong ties. For cohesion perspectives repetition may be an essential ingredient. The accretion of certain impacts may be necessary for one to proceed to the next stage in threshold/critical mass approaches.

The issue of *delivery systems* has received even less attention. Fundamentally, it depends on the operationalization of linkage in any one particular research approach. While both structural equivalence and absorptive capacity approaches would seem to imply some notion of a field, with a mix of different delivery systems, contagion approaches privilege interpersonal contacts.

In some ways, these are very simple approaches, without detailed conceptualizations of *interaction, contraindications*, and *dysfunctions*. So for absorptive capacity, environmental turbulence would seem to be a necessary precondition. If a firm is in a stable environment the relatively high costs associated with the R&D operations may have dysfunctional consequences for the firm. For the strength of weak ties the more embedded one is in the social environment, the more pronounced conforming effects are going to be on the individual. On the other hand, if this environment doesn't provide support and access to people motivated to help, then the individual may be impelled to seek out weak ties. For contagion approaches, the availability of alternative information sources in one's information fields may stabilize resistance and lead to a lack of control on the part of individuals attempting influence. Finally, for threshold and critical mass approaches the level of risk that individuals perceive, in part attributable to a heterogeneous interpersonal environment, may eventually lead to innovation failure.

CHAPTER 7

The World Outside

While this book has focused primarily on communication within organizations, the world outside is often a critical element in determining the level of internal communication. The external environments create imperatives for organizations to learn, to adapt to a changing world. Here I will first review how an organization contextualizes its environment, then turn to the role of individual agents (i.e., boundary spanners) in bringing in information. Then we turn to more traditional conceptions, focusing on how the organization identifies its stakeholders and publics, then engages in systematic efforts to communicate with them, the traditional realms of public relations and advertising, that often use communication campaigns to further their ends.

Contextualizing the World Outside

It has often been noted that more complex organizational environments require more complex internal organizational relationships, especially communicative ones. These environments also provide a critical stimulus for information seeking among organizational members. The environmental scanning that results can substantially increase the volume of information an organization needs to process.[1] Of course, not all organizations will feel the same imperatives to interact with their environment. Emery and Trist have developed a very useful category scheme for analyzing different organizational information environments.[2] They argue that there are four different types: placid, randomized; placid, clustered; disturbed reactive; and turbulent field. *Placid, randomized* organizations have the simplest organizational environment, with no direct competitors or interest groups. Organizations in this category are becoming increasingly rare, and may be only represented by a very few governmental organizations which are no longer relevant to today's environment.

A *placid, clustered* organization has groups in their environment who are interested in their performance, but they do not have direct competitors. Electric utilities, which need to be responsive to customers, government, and environmental groups, would characterize this type of organization. The internal structural arrangements of these organizations change to reflect their environment, with customer relations units, for example, charged with dealing with customers, and with customer service representatives serving as boundary spanners who need to broker queries from customers to the internal organizational environment.

The next two types of organizations identified by Emery and Trist not only need to react to the environment in which they find themselves, they need to become much more proactive in their strategies to uncover information outside their environment and discover means of assimilating it into internal organizational operations. Beyond the structures characteristic of placid-randomized organizations, *disturbed reactive* organizations have to deal with the presence of direct competitors. They must create strategic planning capabilities to optimize their efforts in relation to their environment and potential competitors. They also must create more active ways of discovering what their competitors are doing and what their customers want (e.g., marketing surveys). This concern with reacting and adapting, with an eye to future survivability, naturally puts additional force behind internal communication. These organizations also create specialized public relations and advertising functions that I will return to later in this chapter.

If an organization is not successful in these efforts, then it may find itself in a *turbulent field*, where the organization's ultimate existence is directly threatened. Two types of situations are characteristic of turbulent fields. The first is when the environment of the organization has changed so that the organization's goals are no longer meaningful. For example, while the March of Dimes succeeded in its original goal of fighting polio, if it had not reformulated itself to focus on birth defects, its existence as an organization would have been threatened. In this context, an organization must search its environment for information that will help it, while it is rediscovering who it is and searching the environment for niches in which it can prosper. Obviously, the intensity level of this search is high, since the very survivability of the organization is at stake and the organization may be more willing to take its medicine.

Competitive organizations threatened with takeover or bankruptcy are the second case where elements of the environment are directly threatening the existence of the organization. In this situation, organizations such as Chrysler in the late 1970s and the early 1980s, or General Motors more recently, find that the line separating them from their environment becomes blurred, with elements of their environment increasingly intrusive in internal organizational operations. Chrysler placed a union official on its Board of Directors, and government agencies and banks had effective veto power on decisions relating to the development of product lines.

The proactive strategies necessary for the survival of organizations in disturbed reactive and turbulent field environments generally fall into two classes: placing sensory apparatus into the environment to collect information and deciding what categories of information are vital for the organization to collect. Thus, organizations play a very active role in *enacting* and *contextualizing* their environment.

The first means by which they do this is in their placement of sensory apparatus, scanning and search mechanisms, used to apprehend the world outside. All of us have a *noosphere*, a layer of information that surrounds us, which can be apprehended by our senses.[3] Similarly, organizations place sensors in their environment that allow them to process information. So a competitive organization may: reach out to customers through marketing tools such as telephone or face-to-face mall intercept interviews; have lobbyists roaming the halls of the legislature; have lawyers talking to regulators; have observers outside another organization's research facility; have buyers on site purchasing commodities, and so on. These individuals act as the eyes and ears of the organization; they enable it to experience its environment, and when coupled with correct interpretation, permit an organization to respond adaptively.

The arrangement of an organization's noosphere rests on an organization's interpretation of what are important elements of its environment. Based on this interpretation the organization decides on the placement of resources needed to experience these elements. How the environment is enacted by organizational members determines how information is brought into the organization, but even more importantly it determines what is brought in and how it is likely to be evaluated and then assimilated.[4] An organization's members are likely to only recognize information that they have identified a priori as important and to categorize the information based on their understanding of the world.

If we could reconstruct how the great movie moguls in the 1930s and 1940s reacted to the advent of television, it would provide a useful example of organizations interactions with their environment. They probably read about the invention in the newspapers with some curiosity, but did not perceive it to be the start of a new entertainment medium that would eventually supplant their own. In short, they failed to define adequately what was important in their environment, to conceive of alternative ways of doing their business, and to expand their noosphere to gather detailed information about this phenomenon. An adequate recognition of what was important would have led inevitably to much greater information seeking related to the future development of this new means of communication. In sum, the world outside the organization has many implications for dosage.

There is an increasing tendency to suggest that individuals and groups are not only shaped by context, the classic approach of contingency and situational perspectives, but can in turn shape contexts, if only by how they activate and interpret them. These notions are also revealed in Giddens' arguments concerning the production and reproduction of institutions.[5] In other words, how we perform our roles can change the nature of our institutional contexts. Individuals can only shape contexts if they understand their active ingredients and how they act upon them. In a pragmatic sense, there may be no richer area of study for individuals who desire to shape the world around them (and to understand how they are shaped by it).[6] This has been the traditional function of advertising and public relations.

Karl Weick makes this point forcefully for organizations in his classic concept of the enacted environment, suggesting that instead of organizations responding deterministically to outside stimuli, actors constitute by their actions the environment which they think it is important for them to respond to.[7] Once this environment is constituted then it becomes possible to both reduce uncertainty and to operate in a boundedly rational manner.[8] These processes, then, become critical for insuring careful regulation and monitoring of doses. Indeed, strong ties were negatively associated with performance in highly interconnected strategic alliances in the

highly competitive chip industry. Furthermore, some optimal arrangement of individual strong and weak ties was related to performance in
the semiconductor and steel industries suggesting a classic contingency,
match approach to this problem based on whether a firm was in an exploration versus exploitation environment.[9]

Boundary Spanning

Organizations, as open systems, need to sustain themselves by communicating with diverse and dynamic environments (Box 7.1). The external
communication transferred across organizational boundaries interacts
with the internal flow, affecting structures, procedures and control within
organizations. The interaction with the external environments, often cast
as boundary-spanning activities, has been demonstrated to be an indis-
pensable element for the modern organizations' ability to survive and to
succeed (Aldrich and Herker 1977).[10] These boundary spanners become
the mechanism that operationalizes environmental cues to the internal
organizational structure. These positions are critical to innovations and
the diffusion of ideas between and within organizations. One problem
they can create is imbalances in information within the organization,
with some units of the organization reacting to customer concerns, for
example, while others ignore them.

Box 7.1
Boundary Spanning Over Time

Boundary spanners are the mechanism for bringing information into
the organization. Their numbers and importance interact with such
factors as the number of threats an organization faces as well as the
criticality of their responsiveness to the organization. They, in effect,
can control the amount and frequency of external communication.
The greater their numbers the more the organization must focus on
processing this information if this key resource is not to be wasted.
Unfortunately often boundary spanners find themselves in the position of the fabled messenger in China who gets his head chopped off

(Continued)

(*Continued*)

for bringing the Emperor bad news. Operating at the periphery of social systems often produces a number of dysfunctions including stress, burnout, going native (identifying more with clients than the host organization) and on and on.

One issue that has received only scant empirical attention is the sequencing of information coming into the organization through boundary spanning. Focusing on the Cancer Information Service, three models were tested to explain how boundary-spanning communication develops over time by Johnson and Chang. First, in the functional specialization model, which stresses the formal side of the organization, individuals were posited to focus on either internal or external networks depending on their formal functional positions (e.g., customer service representative). Second, the communication stars explanation suggested that the distinctive external and internal communication roles can be played by the same individual who is predisposed to high levels of communication. While it would seem obvious that there are finite limits to the amount of communication one can engage in, several empirical studies suggest that individuals who are high communicators in one setting are also high in others; that heavy users of one information medium related to work are likely to be users of other media that also carry this same information. This model underlines the informal side of an organization and individual predispositions. Boundary spanners acquire relevant information from their external contacts and filter and feed the information inwardly within the organization. Consequently they are perceived as influential by their peers, who seek them out for information.

A third model offers a cyclical, sequential if you will, explanation of individuals alternating their internal and external communication in a dynamic pattern because of the inevitable systemic, behavioral, and psychological consequences of boundary spanning. Individuals may shift due to the systemic consequences resulting from the boundary-spanning activities and dynamic organizational requirements that, fortunately, could be examined given the longitudinal nature of the data. Strategically, boundary spanners might actively select one network (internal or external) to focus on instead of both networks, to avoid role conflict and to focus their work efforts. So, as suggested by the R&D literature, the importation of external ideas might result in considerable internal communication relating to generating internal innovations, which in turn are then exported to other organizations through external communication.

Johnson and Chang's results suggested a lagged effect, with high levels of internal communication at the preceding time period producing high levels of lagged external communication. In addition to their traditional representational and gatekeeping functions, boundary spanners in this organization also focused on developing community coalitions as a way of building political support from various stakeholders for their ongoing innovation efforts and also as a way of increasing the reach and impact of the organization, thus taking a more proactive role in resource dependence issues. The CIS recognized a central tenet of organizations in competitive environments—they must seek cooperative relationships with other organizations.

Boundary spanners are individuals "who operate at the periphery or boundary of an organization, performing organizational relevant tasks, relating the organization with elements outside it."[11] Adams has identified the following organizational roles as boundary spanners: marketing and sales personnel, purchasing agents, dispatchers and traffic men, personnel recruiters, admission and placement staffs, advertising and public relations workers, information and intelligence gatherers and purveyors, legislative representatives, negotiators and bargaining agents, and so on.[12]

Since organizations must adapt to their environments, a number of formal structures and associated functional roles are created explicitly to deal with them. So, for example, boundary spanners (such as department heads, customer service representatives) maintain external communication because of their formally assigned roles. They are responsible for making communication contacts with external information sources and supplying their colleagues with information concerning the outside environment, all the while maintaining an organization's autonomy. As Johnson and Chang demonstrate, the relationship between internal and external communication can be a complex one (Box 7.1).

Research has focused on boundary functions in terms of the information flowing in interorganizational relationships. Boundary spanners filter and facilitate information flow at an organization's boundary, and they cope with environmental constraints to maintain an organization's autonomy.[13] They "represent an organization to its environments, and the environment to the organization."[14] Thus they play two distinct structural roles: "a gatekeeper, who is a conduit for inflows to the group of which the boundary spanner is a member, and a representative, who is a transmitter of outflows from the group of which the boundary spanner is a member."[15] Tushman and colleagues[15] through their extensive research reinforce the distinction between *gatekeeping* and *representational roles*.[16] Obviously, here we are most interested in gatekeeping functions, since they directly relate to administration of dosages.

Professionals in different organizations share information with each other informally (e.g., TGIFs, association meetings) and formally (e.g., trade journals). The most productive scientists are often those who communicate most outside the boundary of the organization.[17] These positions are critical to innovations and the diffusion of ideas between and within organizations. These boundary spanners become the mechanism that operationalizes environmental cues to the internal organizational structure and they accumulate power in organizations because of their ability to absorb uncertainty. In this sense they may operate as more effective delivery systems because of their more direct linkages to internal structures.

Shaping Our Worlds

While the traditional literature has been concerned with how we react to the world around us, how we contextualize our world is increasingly a central concern of managers. Their efforts should focus on what we enact and what we should pay attention to, as well as more proactively shaping the world so that it's a better match to the organization. So, for example, corporate lobbyists work to create a much more favorable regulatory environment for their organizations.

In today's technology-driven world, in-depth organizational information can be provided with great ease across multiple channels; however, external stakeholder wishes may conflict directly with an organization's willingness to supply such information. In terms of data-sharing, yesterday's inward organizational gaze has been supplanted, to some extent, by today's concerns that sharing certain information could threaten the intellectual property rights of organizations, suggest insider trading issues, create Wikileaks threats, and/or result in legal liabilities. Such concerns greatly inhibit truly participative relations with key stakeholders.

Organizations also are beginning to realize the benefits of closer relationships in a variety of other areas. New ideas and applications have been both proposed and developed by customers themselves. Work forces have been expanded with "volunteers," including citizen scientists who help leverage scant resources by conducting such activities as environmental sampling for state agencies and other nonprofit organizations.

The citizen movement provides another example of the shift in stakeholder involvement, with individuals attempting to influence policy and practice at a number of levels. Citizen journalists, including online bloggers and community radio practitioners, present their work to increasingly large audiences, while citizen scientists who do not agree with organizational and/or governmental assertions often conduct their own testing and analyses, reaching and publicizing independent conclusions. Such individual efforts have expanded into the public relations arena, as well, with individuals using the Internet, and especially social media, to promote their own efforts and causes, sometimes leading to the creation and expansion of viral marketing campaigns.

In the face of such fluid boundaries, the maintenance of stakeholder relationships remains a key issue for organizational management. Stakeholder concerns cut across public–private and corporate–nonprofit sectors, with the mediating role of information transfer from organization to stakeholder at the crux of the relationship. Therefore, managers must choose whether, when, and how to meet the information demands of key stakeholders.

The first step toward making such important decisions, however, is to answer two very important questions:

1. Who is perceived as a legitimate stakeholder, and
2. To what extent should legitimate stakeholder information needs be proactively addressed?

These questions are intimately bound to an organization's adoption of one of three identity orientations: individualistic, relational, or collectivistic.[18] In *individualistic* organizations, decision-making is guided by self-interest. Managers take a pragmatic approach to identifying legitimate primary stakeholders, whose needs are addressed chiefly when there is a direct threat to the organization or some other organizational interest is served. The relative number of acknowledged stakeholders for individualistic organizations tends to be somewhat smaller than those of other identity orientations, while the organization's willingness to provide information will be somewhat reduced. Thus, both the target audience for and amount of information provided will likely be smaller for individualistic organizations.

In contrast, organizations that adopt *relational identity orientations* emphasize the establishment and maintenance of stakeholder partnerships. Such an approach to stakeholder management indicates a somewhat broader view of the relationship between organizations and their stakeholders, implicitly recognizing their symbiotic nature. Relational organizations, therefore, are more likely to perceive a larger number of stakeholders as legitimate and have an increased willingness to provide information to those individuals and groups.

Finally, organizations with *collectivistic identity* orientations speak of themselves in "universal" terms, envisioning themselves as part of a broader network of interested parties. These organizations incorporate pro-social goals into their agendas and see themselves as one of many stakeholders involved in larger processes. These commitments drive collectivistic organizations to provide information widely to broader publics.

Each of the three identity orientations points to different perceptions of stakeholder legitimacy and varying organizational willingness to provide information and the determination of an appropriate dose and therapeutic agent. An individualistic organization that supplies limited information to stakeholders who have little desire for additional information may have less need to adapt its strategy than a collectivistic organization freely sharing vast amounts of information with stakeholders.

As interrelationships among organizations and individuals become increasingly complex, so too must organizations develop more complex ways of building and maintaining goodwill in those relationships. Organizations must be ever more attuned to their environment, especially when concerns arise about the potentially disruptive impact of some innovations on their operations and stakeholder relationships. Managers therefore face a daunting task in today's rapidly expanding, ever-changing information environment: providing the necessary amount of information that meet stakeholder needs. Stakeholders, in turn, must come to intelligent judgments about an organization and its operations based on the welter of facts, forecasts, gossip, and intuition that makes up their information environment, the general thrust of modern organizations is to be more responsive and adaptive to external stakeholders.

Public Relations

It is important for organizations to effectively match their stakeholders' needs in the amount and types of information that they make available. One way in which to navigate the complexities of modern organization–stakeholder relationships and the resulting impacts on flow of information from the organization to the stakeholder is to implement a *co-orientation* approach to the issue. Originating in psychology to illustrate the relationship between psychological balance and mutual benefit,[19] co-orientation models have been adopted by public relations professionals as tools for understanding relationships between organizations and their stakeholders.[20] Since the model can be adapted to the specific challenges of organization–stakeholder information matching, organizations can identify their own placement within the four conditions of mismatch and match, thus being better positioned to adapt information strategies and improve stakeholder satisfaction.

For this co-orientation approach to work, managers must determine exactly who the organization's stakeholders are, thus helping identify what types of information are needed as stakeholder interests and information needs are closely coupled. In general, stakeholders support organizational functioning, whether by providing labor, financial support, a potential market, positive exposure, or some other function. Stakeholder typologies distinguish between primary stakeholders, whose role is essential to organizational survival, and secondary stakeholders, who are not essential to survival but whose actions, nevertheless, can affect the organization.[21]

Modern public relations approaches stress the development of long-term relationships through various processes associated with relationship building. Some public relations practitioners serve as representational boundary spanners explaining their organization to the outside world while developing a sensitivity to the needs of stakeholders outside. One popular approach to public relations is that developed by the Grunig's in the *Organization–Public Relationships* (ORP) theory.[22] This approach identifies several antecedents to successful ORP including such issues as established homophily, in part through networking, between the organization and stakeholders. The public relations practitioner also needs to establish access to the organization's leadership encouraging them to have a dialectical approach to conflict management through openness and transparency. Public relations practitioners attempt to stress the communal nature of the enterprise—both the organization and stakeholder having similar goals, leading to higher trusts more commitment and control mutuality.

Thus in a *situational theory of the public* approach, much as in the tailoring approach to campaigns we will soon turn to, segmenting becomes important, especially identifying those elements of the public who share an interest in the organization and its goals. *Hot issue publics* are highly focused and involved on particular issues such as the environment. Next comes the *aware public* followed by *latent publics* and *nonpublics* who are completely uninvolved with the organization and what it seeks to accomplish. These segmentations determine whether:

- the public will actively process and seek further information dealing with an issue;
- perceive the importance of the problem;
- believe in the existence of constraints and barriers to action; and

- ultimately determine their level of involvement with the object or issues.

All of these factors take on an increased importance when the public believes there is a risk involved in the organizations activities. *Risk communication* often fundamentally relates to uncertainty, particularly concerning matters of health. *Crisis communication* is a special branch of risk communication that implies high salience and an immediate response is needed to particular concerns. In general *risk communication* has focused on *three levels*:

- correcting personally risky behavior which is often the focus of communication campaigns;
- communicating risk at an interpersonal level, such as genetic counseling which is again beyond our purview; and
- communicating risk to the public at large.

How corporations handle crises can be company altering events. Classically, the literature has referred to Johnson & Johnson's handling of the Tylenol tampering episode with rapid response at considerable cost to the organization creating an image of Johnson & Johnson that has endured.[23] Covello has articulated several *best practices* for handling these sorts of events:

- listen to and partner was stakeholders in part, to determine what they already know;
- establish, build and maintain trust;
- work with media;
- develop an appropriate message based on your understanding of the needs of the media and the public; and
- engage in honest clear and compassionate communication that is thoughtful.[24]

The Holy Grail for a public relations practitioner is to develop messages that reduce the gap between perceived risk and actual probabilistic risk. Public relations practitioners in today's Internet age also need to be concerned about social amplification processes where messages quickly become viral and take on a life of their own that are difficult to control.

Contemporary views of communication are more likely to stress a dialogic view of interaction, both parties initiating and attending to messages in turn. Professionals' most important role in these more modern perspectives is as stimulus or cue to action, defining the agenda of the most important issues that an audience needs to face.

Traditionally, managers have approached stakeholder communication via a one-way, top-down flow of communication. They have relied on mass media campaigns to reach large numbers of people efficiently. Many approaches and assumptions of traditional media research often were implicit in this approach. Somewhat akin to mass media's historical bullet theory, stakeholders were thought to be a relatively passive, defenseless audience whose input was only sought through surveys or focus groups to determine the best way of changing their minds and their subsequent behaviors.

All this points to the benefits of corporation adopting easy-to-use push technologies that "guide" consumers, as well as using multiple channels, or delivery systems to reach stakeholders. Following the traditional top–down approach to stakeholder communication, organizational websites provide one point of stakeholder exposure to information; however, unlike traditional media channels, such websites have dialogic capabilities. Organizations can use their official online presence to gather information from stakeholders, ranging from basic demographic data to concerns and priorities elicited through online surveys. Organizations also can implement social networking approaches to supplement these efforts, not only to provide information but also to build relationships with stakeholders, providing another arena in which the "temperature" of stakeholder information needs can be taken. Further, organizations can expand the recipients of official communications, such as press releases and annual reports, to include more nontraditional targets, including citizen journalists, respected and relevant blogs, and citizen science groups.

As made explicit earlier in this chapter, it is important that the information provided by organizations meets the perceived needs of stakeholders to the greatest extent possible. By providing the right amount of information to the right stakeholders, organizations can contribute to a state of shared *Satisfaction* in the information exchange; striving for a match within contingent frameworks. However, when a mismatch occurs, states of *Adversarialism* or *Inundation* can arise, reducing stakeholder satisfaction and potentially harming the organization's operations. Even when information supply and demand are matched, there is the potential for relationship devolution if either stakeholder needs or organizational willingness to supply information change without a complementary shift from the other party. Thus, it is key that managers continually scan their organizations' stakeholders, partly through the actions of boundary spanners, to determine the desired level of information sought, along with making internal determinations about which information can be safely shared, establishing information architectures that satisfy stakeholder information needs and which, in the process satisfy an organization's strategic goals. A focus on dialogue and public relations increases the receptivity of messages used in communication campaigns.

Campaigns

The traditional approach to administrative communication with publics that most clearly encapsulates the dosage metaphor is that related communication campaigns, most often associated with advertising;[25] campaign professionals attempt to achieve a clearly specified change in an audience, especially at a group level, during a limited period of time.[26]

> Campaign evaluators often compare those exposed and not exposed to a campaign in order to examine whether a campaign had its intended effects. These types of analyses essentially adopt a dose–response point of view in which those with greater exposure to a campaign are theorized to adopt greater behavioral changes than those who receive less exposure.[27]

This is the most scientifically advanced area of dosage research in communication (at least in terms of quantitative approaches). In part, because the desired outcome and the therapeutic agents are so clear, traditionally campaign professionals have thought of these processes in terms of a one-way, top–down flow of communication. They have relied on the mass media to reach large numbers of people efficiently in their campaigns (e.g., increasing sales). These authoritative dicta and the lack of interactivity in the communication channel, or delivery system, were meant as much to discourage dialogue as to stimulate it. However, there is a commonplace recognition now that mediated channels alone are unlikely to have the desired impacts, they must be supplemented with interpersonal communication within social networks.[28]

In part, because of the growing availability of federal funds for health-related communication campaigns, the decades of the 1960s and 1970s saw a resurgence of interest in campaigns and a feeling that they can succeed in certain circumstances. Interestingly this resulted in blame for unsuccessful campaigns being shifted from the recipients of the messages to the designers of the campaign.[29] Notable research during the early 1970s included the Stanford Three Community Study and later the Five City Project,[30] which more carefully segmented the audience along such factors as obesity. This latter study more carefully operationalized issues relating to dosage and its linkage to actual campaign effects: "… remembered message percentages showed how the specification of the 'dose' of the intervention can increase your understanding of the 'response' in campaign outcomes."[31]

The current era of communication campaign research has been labeled the *conditional effects era* in which principles of effective campaigns have been formalized and numerous examples of successful campaigns illustrate how they can creatively be put into action.[32] The dosage metaphor is clearly revealed in *successful campaign principles*:

- increase exposure,
- develop properly targeted messages, and
- deliver them frequently.

Underlying the early campaign approach was the idea that communication in effect could be "shot" into an audience.[33] However, most campaigns must grapple with the fact that they do not really reach intended audiences and therefore they do not succeed among a large number of their audience members.[34] Communicators have learned that these classic approaches are not very effective unless the needs of the audience and their reaction to messages are considered. Thus, it soon became apparent that, while there were some notable successes, audiences could be remarkably resistant to campaigns, especially when they did not correspond to the views of their immediate social network.[35] Indeed, campaigns tend to reach those who are already interested and typically bypass those who are most in need of their messages.[36] In effect campaigns reach the already converted. While this might have a beneficial effect of further reinforcing beliefs, the audience members who are most in need of being reached are precisely those members who are least likely to attend to messages.[37]

Campaigns often fail because their recommended beneficial effects are not apparent and they do not identify market segments within the total audience who require different communication approaches in line with their specific needs. The bottom line issue is that interested people acquire on their own most of the information available on any subject.[38] The more scarce a piece of information is, the more one must work on their own to obtain it, typically the more valued and persuasive it tends to be.[39] Prepackaged campaigns fail to realize some people are active information seekers and they do not answer the very specific questions active seekers have.[40] This suggests that finer grain discriminations of the audience may be necessary to insure effective communication; much as in emerging approaches to personalized medicine.

As we have seen, perhaps the best strategy is to achieve a "match" between the information carriers chosen to disseminate information and the desired outcomes. Thus, the question becomes the much more sophisticated one of placing the most appropriate content, in the most appropriate channel, where it is most likely to be used by a predetermined audience. So, contemporary approaches to tailoring offer the promise of systematically measuring dosage amounts and proper sequencing of messages.[41]

McGuire has also pointed out the very low probabilities of success of communication campaigns given the long string of steps that must be fulfilled (e.g., first get the audience's attention), each of which only has moderate probability of success.[42] It is now recognized, the average health communication campaign changes the behavior of about 8 percent of the population;[43] or stated in another way, the average media campaign effect represented by the mean of correlations in a meta-analysis was 0.09.[44]

This line of thought also introduces notions of the relative cost-effectiveness of various approaches to campaigns. For example, systematic comparisons of smoking cessation, comparing the clinical model, which was largely interpersonal, and the public health model, which is community-based found much different quit rates, with a clinical approach, which had intensive multisession interventions, with trained professionals, nearly twice as effective. However, the cost per individual reached is also much higher in this approach.[45] This sort of calculation has typically resulted in the cost conscious campaign administrators choosing the mass media for campaigns since in the end more people can be reached resulting in a greater yield of changes in targeted behavior. Another representative line of research in this area, found campaign costs over a 2-year period about a dollar per 11 packs not smoked. Further, the study suggested that for each 10 percent increase in media time purchased, at a cost of about $2 million at the time, produced an additional decline of 0.5 percent in cigarette sales.[46] In Massachusetts, where over $50 million was spent in a 4-year campaign, or about $8 per capita, there was evidence for reduction of smoking initiation among youths.[47] Analyses of this sort are quite common in the commercial world, but proprietary, considerably retarding the development of a science of dosage.

Unfortunately, systematic comparisons of different approaches to delivering messages do not clearly indicate that more sophisticated expensive and complicated approaches always result in better outcomes.[48] Outcomes of safety campaigns in organizations suggest that practitioners have better outcomes when messages are kept simple; too many specific details, safety rules, and safety procedures can actually result in diminished performance.[49] One clear instance in which "more is usually better" across a number of interventions is that greater interpersonal contact over longer periods of time produces superior results.[50]

Conclusion

Campaigns traditionally have been the primary communication strategy for influencing the world outside; one that is intimately tied to the dosage metaphor.

Exposure is a necessary, but not a sufficient, condition for change in the target population.[51]

What is the impact of various quantities of campaign messages? Research should examine (a) the minimum volume of stimuli needed to achieve meaningful effects on key outcomes and (b) the quantitative point of diminishing returns from larger volumes.[52]

So, earlier approaches to campaigns did not focus in a detailed or sophisticated way on amount and frequency elements of the dosage metaphor. Such campaigns fail because:

- They neglect basic elements of the dosage metaphor such as ensuring widespread, frequent, and prolonged exposure to messages.
- They do not focus on audience segmentation, a version of personalized medicine, or targeting.[53]
- In terms of sequencing, how long a campaign should last to achieve effects is also a great unknown; as is the point at which a message reaches diminishing returns in terms of its repetition.[54]
- A major focus of some public communication campaigns is also to encourage people to seek other channels for information achieving both variety in delivery systems and repetition of messages.[55] So cues to action are followed by appropriate mental processing, which then leads to health behaviors, and stages of change go through a predictable progression. A great unknown, relating to campaign sequencing effects is their decay rate,[56] which is also a classic issue related to dosage impacts, with parallels to the flushing of drugs from the system, and a very important consideration when a behavior that is advocated by a campaign (e.g., breast self-exams) later turns out to be not as efficacious as first thought.
- As in so many of the communication phenomenon we have examined, contraindications focus on issues of match. So unwillingness to change, the wrong stage, and poor audience segmentation all can lead to failed campaigns.

Beyond the wasted resources devoted to poorly designed campaigns there has been little consideration of dysfunctional aspects of campaign approaches: perhaps because of their implicit roots in administrative science and a general feeling that those in authority know what's best. However, repeated reliance on campaigns fosters a climate of dependency and a presumption that those in power know best, undercutting individual autonomy and initiative. As in any paternalistic approach, there are general problems with campaigns top–down approach resulting in passive or dependent reactive audiences who do not engage in "intelligent noncompliance."

CHAPTER 8

Summing Up

We started this work by focusing on fundamentals. After the introduction of dosage in Chapter 1, Chapter 2 focused on expanding the metaphor of dosage, detailing its many elements, as well as discussing generally the uses and limits of metaphor. A substantial advantage of examining the dosage metaphor is its application to communication across a number of levels of analysis. Naturally, given its historically pragmatic focus, organizational communication theorists have concentrated on issues that could be related to dosage and, most interestingly, have often explicitly used metaphors as a basis for their conceptualizations. Chapter 3 detailed the right match between communication efforts and desired outcomes primarily reflected in communication channel research, differentiation and integration, and technology and structure.

The most elementary of communication contexts is that focusing on relationships between two people in interpersonal communication. Chapter 4 detailed some of the more interesting findings relating to supervisor–subordinate communication relationships, a surrogate for a wide range of dyadic relationships where there are asymmetric status and power differences. Chapter 5 discussed the fundamental issues of load and of cost–benefit analyses relating to dosage dealing with productivity. Chapter 6 focused on perhaps the most contemporaneously interesting issue of change. Highlighted network analysis concepts included the strength of weak ties, structural equivalence, and social contagion. Chapter 7 focused on the organizations relationship with the world outside, focusing on public relations and the associated issues of communication campaigns.

The final chapter analyzes the dosage metaphor in broad sweep and suggested maxims for a contrarian, minimalist approach to management.

Analyzing the Dosage Metaphor

This section comprehensively assesses the application of the dosage metaphor to managerial communication remembering: "It is the dose that makes a poison," runs an old adage in medicine ....[1] Perhaps the best place to start is to systematically review the application of the elements of the dosage metaphor. One set of interrelated issues for these elements is the notion of the separability and rigorous applications of amount, frequency and sequencing. Certainly in testing drugs these issues are distinct and develop different recommendations depending on their impacts. So one takes a medication one time a day with a certain number of milligrams following a meal. After this course of treatment another medication is introduced with similar prescriptions as to amount and frequency. There is a range of options for these different applications that is almost infinite. So one shot of a particular vaccine, somewhat reminiscent of hypodermic needle or magic bullet approaches, can be sufficient to achieve particular purposes such as the prevention of polio. At other times, a continuous flow of treatment, such as intravenous fluids, is the best way to administer a particular drug.

Very few communication theories even begin to approach this level of sophistication.[2] Perhaps the ones that are the closest are campaign researchers who, in their very sophisticated designs, are concerned with amount issues in terms of things like the raw value of media buys, with frequency issues in terms of the period of time necessary to achieve particular impacts; and with sequencing issues for things like the decay of impact of any one particular message, first raising awareness of the need to change before suggesting exactly what kind of change is efficacious. At least theoretically, there also is the suggestion within the interpersonal approaches of an appreciation for the interplay between these three elements. So at the outset of the relationship someone may preliminarily test the waters with self-disclosures of a more intimate nature, if this is met with approval and reciprocity, then successively more intimate and frequent self-disclosures may follow.

Similarly, there is a range within communication theory of sophistication in terms of approaches to delivery systems. For some approaches, such as media richness, there is considerable appreciation for the different impacts associated with the means of delivering a communication message. Other approaches narrowly limit themselves to one medium, which is particularly true of mass media and interpersonal scholars, even though in the world of the Internet the really fascinating issue is how these two approaches are being blended. Delivery systems also entail precision in the targeting of potential therapeutic agents. So one of the hottest issues in oncology is the more focused application of chemotherapy agents which are highly toxic. The less "leakage" there is of the intended agent to other vital biological systems, the more intense the treatment can become.

Interactions and contraindications both deal with factors that may affect the outcomes of particular dosages. Interactions generally modify the impact of particular therapeutic agents, so messages from a trustworthy source that are delivered interpersonally may have a much greater impact than messages from a source with whom we have a guarded relationship that are delivered by mediated channels. On the other hand, contraindications indicate situations where giving any dose at all might be inappropriate. Interactions, at least in terms of issues relating to contingency theory and inappropriate matches of agents to problems, have received considerable attention. Perhaps, because of the taken for granted presumption that communication is inherently beneficial, much less attention has been paid to contraindications of dosage.

The dysfunctional impacts of dosages have also received minimal attention within communication for similar reasons. In part, because of a familiar presumption in diffusion of innovation research that communication is an inherent good people who resisted it were often seen in very negative terms.[3] However, we now live in a much more skeptical age, where even the most seemingly beneficial of prescriptions often come with a price tag of which we are unaware. In the communication literature, historically this was perhaps best revealed in the ideology of openness and the self-disclosure literature. It is now widely recognized that openness is not a universal good and that it can actually harm relationships.

The concept of match also highlights dysfunctions in terms of inappropriate use of resources and even the potential for increasing conflict and misunderstandings in organizational settings when too many integrating mechanisms are used. It's sometimes better to let sleeping dogs lie. As a result of a greater prevalence of critical scholars working on mass media related issues, there is somewhat more of an appreciation for larger societal impacts in the operation of mass media. So, for example, political scientists are increasingly concerned with the implications of the fragmentation of people into separate interest groups, which entail selective exposure, on the polity's larger democratic participation.

Often dysfunctional views emerge when a metaphor is explored at a deeper level. So one may start out with a surface metaphor of an organization as one big happy family and only on deeper reflection uncovers family feuds, sibling rivalry, nepotism, and in-law relationships.[4] A wide variety of ethical and/or dysfunctional issues are associated with the dosage metaphor. Recognition of the following six issues can assist us in understanding the darker side of communication relationships.

1. Historically the field has paid little attention to issues of inertia and the lingering impacts of communication. While the necessity of flushing out harmful drugs is widely recognized in pharmaceutical applications, it has received scant attention within communication.[5] This is also true for issues relating to the creation of dependent relationships and withdrawal from them. Are some aspects of communication addictive? If so, what is our equivalent of a substance abuse program?

2. In some cases the amount of the dose may be so large as to be impracticable, of such profound consequences that you are in effect killed by the cure. It also may be the case that small doses have no impacts—only really dramatic changes produce results. This also may be similar to a true believer, radical point that, how do you know our ideology doesn't work, it has never really been tried in practice.

3. Sometimes treatment masks symptoms, interfering with correct diagnosis. For example, I was recently the victim of ehrlichiosis following a tick bite, a rather exotic occurrence. In spite of repeatedly pointing to the remnants of the tick bite with various doctors, it was presumed that I had some other type of bacterial infection so a course of a powerful, broad spectrum antibiotic was prescribed which lowered my high fever and dampened my other symptoms. But when I left for vacation my original symptoms shortly returned

with a vengeance. In organizations an analogy might be using pay and fringe benefits to mask underlying causes of low morale. Stirring rhetoric can also deflect our attention away from deeper problems.

4. Some might worry that a science of dosage offers the possibility of enhanced manipulation of audiences. Unfortunately this already exists in the commercial world, it is just hidden from public view, often by proprietary research programs. So, a greater understanding of the issues surrounding dosage within the public domain may allow us to act in a countervailing way to messages that might be inherently troublesome. Relatedly, we need a code of ethics for dosage practitioners in communication.

5. Do we have an approach for people who self-prescribe communication remedies? Certainly the self-prescribing of performance-enhancing drugs has become a pandemic. So, it has become increasingly normative behavior for college students to use performance-enhancing Adderall and other attention deficit drugs to focus their attention in their studies. Do we want organizations full of people on the mental equivalent of steroids?

6. Can everyone really afford a dose? Is there the equivalent of nationalized medicine? As in all things you get what you can pay for. Can everyone afford a communication dose? One of the great public policy issues of our times is related to the financing of political campaigns and equating them to "free" speech issues. If not everyone has access to the same possibilities for delivering (e.g., buying air time for commercials) messages, what does this mean for our public discourse?

Finally, as in all metaphors one must be careful. We do not want to emulate the medicalization model where everyone is ill, that is primarily reactive. We may want more of a wellness approach, somewhat like positive psychology, that focuses on preventive medicine.

Metaphor qua Metaphor

Metaphors can be analyzed as a whole by their depth, breadth, interrelationships, and coherence.[6] First, in terms of depth does the metaphor approach the level of tacit understanding of a root metaphor in its symbolic manifestations? Certainly at a naïve level all of us have a fundamental understanding of dosage or a dose. Hopefully this work has demonstrated at more than a surface level multiple manifestations of dosage in a variety of communication contexts and theories and that thinking about communication with this metaphor rings true and resonates.

In some ways the issue of depth relates to the extent to which a metaphor has been conventionalized; or is it a readily accepted means of describing any phenomena? For example, the organization as machine metaphor is one that has been deeply conventionalized.[7] One test of this is to ask is it difficult to even think of a phenomenon without evocation of the metaphor? "Meaningful metaphors" are discovered, rather than created; they reflect the "metaphors in use,"[8] they are also particularly "live."[9] I have attempted here to uncover the pervasiveness of the dosage metaphor in our thought, to reveal that it is tacitly conventionalized in many theories of communication, especially those focusing on issues of intimacy, exposure, and change.

Second, in terms of breadth, at least in terms of the number of contexts in which it operates, dosage is a wide-ranging metaphor. However, it certainly doesn't encompass all of communication behavior or all theories of communication, especially those more concerned with deeper levels of the development of meaning and associated symbols, the content of the message if you will, the very essence of therapeutic agents. Sadly though, since all the social sciences have given up any hope of a grand theory that explains everything, the question becomes is the coverage of dosage sufficient to make it an interesting approach to communication?

Third, the different components, or elements, of the definition of dosage are strongly interrelated with each other. So, for example, the amount of a therapeutic agent that is given is somewhat limited by available delivery systems.

Finally, coherence suggests a thematic integrity to the metaphor; that it hangs together in an integrated way. Hopefully our attention to the elements of the dosage metaphor indicates that this is so.

Yet another way of evaluating the dosage metaphor is in terms of its heuristic value. At least on its face, dosage is a simple, elegant, and parsimonious way of approaching communication problems and issues. However, it may not be aesthetically appealing to many because of its strong roots in medical approaches and its linkage to administrative science. This, when coupled with its linear, top–down feel for many who have a relatively naïve understanding of the metaphor may result in a near visceral reaction to its application to communication. So, for example, even doctors, through blood tests, continue to monitor the impacts of dosages on patients and receive feedback, adjusting future doses of therapeutic agents accordingly. In an interesting way, it is the dosage metaphor's roots in scientific approaches that allow us to explain, predict, and control, the traditional criteria for any theoretical approach, may exacerbate this reaction from some.

Perhaps the most telling test of the application of this metaphor is its ability to clarify, provide understanding, and guide observation of problems that interest both practitioners and researchers.[10] A useful metaphor should allow us to apply something we know about to enrich our understanding of its target. Hopefully, I have demonstrated that the dosage metaphor allows us to see things in a new light to make manifest things that were only tacit, and then easily communicate them to others. Such a process often evokes more resonance in the mind of the other than the words alone would explain, thus allowing us to communicate more effectively, providing an interpretive framework for the other.

> Without considering audience attributes there is a greater likelihood that receivers will ignore the message, misunderstand the content, reject applicability to self, challenge claims with counterarguments, or derogate the source ....[11]

While this is seldom actually realized, the study of the metaphor should enrich the understanding of both the phenomenon to which it is applied and the underlying metaphor itself. What can communication scholars contribute to our understanding of dosage? Perhaps our greatest contribution can come in greater understanding of audience reaction/receptivity issues which is the growing trend in personalized medicine. Supposedly, our field from its beginning has been interested in both the source and receiver of communication messages. However, communication research and theory have been dominated by a source perspective, primarily related to the field's obsession with persuasion.[12] By and large, except for some cognitive difficulties individuals might have in processing messages, the nature and motives of receivers have been downplayed or ignored. Implicitly our conventionalized understanding of communication through application of the conduit metaphor has trivialized the role of receivers in doing the hard work of reconstructing messages that are sent to them.[13] If receivers have been examined, it usually is in the context of how we can better get our messages across to them. So, we focus on the imperfections in receivers, particularly their cognitive limits. We also dwell on the question of what do receivers "really want anyway?," so that we can construct more effective persuasive communication campaigns.[14]

As we have seen one historical reason for problems in communication campaigns has been a failure to consider a complete range of the motivations that impel individual actors. This has in turn led to perceptions of an obstinate and irrational audience that is blamed for thwarting well-meaning and beneficial campaigns. (People just don't understand what's good for them!). Focusing on preparing a message often leads managers astray, because the assumption is just because a message is uttered, it is attended to. Relatedly, physicians are continually astonished about the lack of adherence to medical doses of pharmaceuticals. However, how a message is perceived really determines the nature of a communication event and receivers are ultimately the arbiters of the value of any piece of information.[15] It is the audience that ultimately interprets any message[16] and, more basically, determines whether any communication will occur.[17]

An approach that has receivers as its focus inherently tries to picture the world of the actor and the self-interests that motivate him/her to particular behaviors.[18] But individuals, of course, are not totally free of constraints which govern their actions. They depend on others for information and for services and the general societal framework in which they are embedded restricts the range of questions and alternatives that can be pursued. As the classic selective perception and selective attention literatures suggest,[19] a fundamental property of communication relationships is that a receiver must attend to a communication message for any communication to occur.[20] In a somewhat similar way, one of the fundamental understudied problems of medical approaches is that patients often administer dosages in ways that diminish their impact because of costs, side-effects, and so on.

Greater appreciation of the centrality of the dosage metaphor can help make communication more relevant to the world of practice. Communication purists who resist reducing the complexities of communication to a formula should understand the frustration that this produces in practitioners and how they will cope with it. If we do not respond to their needs they will turn to scoundrels who offer them patent medicines because their problems are compelling and demand solutions.

A Minimalist Approach to Managerial Communication

The best way to improve managerial communication is not to produce more information, but to reduce the amount of information any one subsystem must process.[21] Increasingly the ability to focus and to develop coherent approaches to an increasingly complex world may be the most useful approach. For example, lower levels of face-to-face communication had many impacts for teleworkers: fewer distractions, less involvement in office politics, and greater job satisfaction.[22] As we have also noted, Hansen and Haas found an interesting paradox in knowledge markets—the less information a supplier provided the more it was used, because of a reputation the supplier developed for focus and quality.[23]

As I noted at the outset of this work, there has been a communication metamyth that more is necessarily better. As a result we do not have measured approaches to problems. We do not know when to stop, and perhaps like a doctor who gives someone a drug because they expect it, in our consulting roles we are often pressed to do something. What is our equivalent of the "effective dose" concept in medicine—the smallest amount of a substance needed to produce a measurable effect? It has been suggested that one approach to designing interventions would be to start with the minimal intervention needed for change, and only when this proved to be unsuccessful to proceed to more expensive, complicated interventions.[24]

Ten Maxims

Let us now turn then to our top 10 list of maxims which should govern a manager who is attuned to a minimalist approach to dosage.

Focus Attention

In Chapter 5 I discussed how management must focus the attention of organizational members on key issues, which they often do through agenda setting processes related to goal setting and visioning. A manager's most important role is as a stimulus or cue to action. They must define the most important issues that an organization needs to face.[25] Many observers have commented that attention rather than information is the scarce resource in organizations[26]; fundamentally we must accept human limits to information processing. Some people have just reached a saturation point; they cannot spend any more time communicating.[27] But there is always a demand to do more, to recognize key threats in the environment, for example, by actively contextualizing or expanding one's noosphere. While more and more information can be produced more efficiently, there is a concomitant increase in the costs of consuming (e.g., interpreting, analyzing) this information. Someone who is already overloaded will not be ready to receive new information unless they can easily recognize its significance and assimilate it into an existing framework. *By setting an agenda a manager prepares his audience for future doses, promoting receptivity.*

Develop Complementary Routines

The impact of therapeutic agents is often determined by how they interact with other related factors. So high blood pressure medicines work best when complemented by weight loss and dietary changes. Similarly, managers must ensure that they have methods in place that capture their vision; established routines, structures, frameworks, and planning put in place that minimizes the need for communication and reinforces any messages that are delivered.

A manager must have a clear idea of where she/he is going and establish routine procedures that facilitate achieving their goals. The key differences in approach come in the manner in which the manager responds cybernetically to information suggesting departures from routines and goals. The classic micromanager approach will have the manager very closely supervising the behavior of his/her employees to ensure that there are no deviations. The manager also engages in various near Machiavellian

strategies to ensure that there are no competing goals and visions developing within the part of the organization under their control.

Minimalist managers recognize that there is more than one way to
skin a cat in the traditions of equifinality; they realize that there are multiple ways in which goals can be accomplished and many different routines that will satisfy them. They also allow for greater range in outcome
related behaviors; since this ultimately results in future improvements in
the system. Naturally, this requires a fair amount of faith and trust on
the part of the manager. This faith and trust is increased in the selection
and socialization processes that the manager has implemented. For this
approach to work, the manager must select good people and ensure that
they have a clear idea of where the organization is heading.

Don't Dictate, Delegate

Firms increasingly should be organized as knowledge specialists and professionals reacting to a common theme, emulating many characteristics of
symphony orchestras.[28] In orchestras there must be some common thread
that all the members are working from if their individual efforts are not to
become too discordant. Some simplifying melody is required so that the
players can react to and build on them in their solo performances, upon
which the whole effort depends. In this way, minimalist organizations
often have an advantage in adapting to organizational change.[29]

"Only the most arrogant of leaders will insist on personally making all the critical decisions in an organization that lives on specialized
knowledge."[30] New workplace innovations fail when management refuses
to relinquish centralized control which prevents local adaptation.[31] The
most appropriate role for a manager is to provide a rudder, steering
the larger enterprise in the right direction, but allowing the others in the
work to do the other tasks necessary to get there.

In some ways traditional views of management, with an emphasis
on anticipating problems, documenting them, and ultimately controlling them,[32] are antithetical to effectiveness. Managers govern best by
letting go. If you have given people space and they accomplish things
pretty much on their own, you also have to be willing to insure they get
appropriate share of credit.

Good Followership Is as Important as Leadership

Paying attention to good followership is essential to leadership,[33] especially if a manager pays attention to the first three maxims and allows others to do their work for them when they delegate their tasks. Spending your time up front selecting good people is the wisest thing a leader can do.

Some people are all too ready to follow orders; they want someone to do their thinking for them. Their first question is what does the manager want rather than what they think they should do. Most importantly, these followers do not serve as an effective corrective when a leader chooses to engage in a foolish or unwise course of action—they are more than willing to follow them over the cliff!

However, if your boss is a micromanager, it is hard to resist infection. The dark side spreads quickly.

Look for Butterflies

A manager should think first about how one can get others to do their work for them. This is essentially the inspiration behind viral marketing campaigns, and is one of the principles behind therapeutic agents where a small dose of the agent, given in the right delivery system, stimulates or provokes the body's own immune systems to do the intended work. As Duncan Watts has ably pointed out, to achieve certain contagion effects, volume may not be the issue; but who or what groups are "infected" and "percolating" the change, because of their centrality, may be more critical.[34] Whenever possible set the agenda, allow other processes to do the work; look for butterfly impacts where very small impacts reverberate through a system to ultimately have very pronounced impacts on it as a whole.

Be Patient, Allow Time for Things to Work

It takes time for results, very few drugs work immediately, instantaneously. A watched pot seldom boils. When confronted with pressing problems it is difficult to sit back and wait for the medicine to work. But some medications need to build up to certain levels before they will work. Similarly, some innovations need to reach a critical mass before they truly kick in. So, a new communication system does not become effective until a sufficient proportion of communicators start using it.

An Apple a Day Keeps the Doctor Away

It is better to prevent a problem, then to solve it once it is manifested. It is much less glamorous to be an internist or general practitioner, whose patents are counseled into healthy life styles, than to be a surgeon who heroically saves a patient through open heart surgery. Some more unscrupulous managers may manufacture crises, so that they can demonstrate their indispensability. However, it requires much less effort, and certainly less drama, to foresee problems and deal with them in such a way that they never do become manifest. The ultimate in productivity is no medicine at all, which also means no downside risk of dysfunctional side effects; or at the very least allow one to take a less dangerous, more palatable medicine.

Thoughtful Forgetting Is as Important as Remembering

Due to interaction effects it is sometime necessary to flush drugs from one's system, eliminating the influence of the old before starting the new. Of course, one needs to think carefully about what information should be excluded from an organization's existing knowledge base. Knowledge disavowal is an important organizational process, it allows for the dismissal of disconfirming ideas and the recognition of ideas as not fully formed (or at least not developed enough to overturn conventional organizational wisdom) and is one way of coping with information overload.[35] How long do we hold on to an answer we struggled so hard to attain? How an organization goes about forgetting is a critical issue.[36]

The Less You Have to Say the Better

Govern with parables, metaphors that are rich and can be translated to many different contexts. These parables require some active participation on the part of receivers to be applied to new contexts activating cognitive processes in receivers that otherwise might atrophy.

Most attempts to motivate workers are dysfunctional. Expending energy to motivate people is largely a waste of time—rather managers should focus on insuring their actions are to not de-motivating people.[37] The more directions you give, the more concretely you give them, the more workers will become reactive, not proactive.

Saying less also has some additional benefits. Just as when rules multiply barrack lawyers can search for unexpected interactions and inconsistences[38] and actually have more potential ways of choosing the course of action they desire. The more you say the more workers can pick and choose what they will act on; "… some administrators adapt the attitude that the less they say, the less they can be misinterpreted."[39]

Give Only the Medication That Is Needed

What is our equivalent of "effective dose" concept in medicine—the smallest amount of a substance needed to produce a measurable effect? The American cultural metamyth that more is necessarily better has meant that we do not have measured approaches to problems. We do not know when to stop, and perhaps like a doctor who gives someone a drug because they expect one, we are often pressed to do something. Not every problem can be solved, especially by communication. Like the constant, ubiquitous use of antibiotics building up the resistance of the bugs they are meant to fight, constant messaging can lead to reduced impacts of messages when they might be most needed.

Conclusion

Of course, there are situations in which a minimalist approach is not likely to work. Especially in a chaotic environment that is rapidly changing, a manager may be compelled to act forcefully and unilaterally, hoping people will rally around the flag. There are also institutional forces that often require a cult of personality surrounding a leader. This is becoming increasingly true in academe where attracting resources either from private donors or from state legislators rests on a charismatic vision of a president or dean. Often leader advancement and promotion rests on the buck stopping with them. There are also often grave personal consequences for the actions of followers. In these circumstances it is very difficult for any human being to truly delegate.

Especially early on, managers are often confronted by an existing team that they had little role in selecting. They must confront the problem of unscrupulous followers with their own agenda—embezzlers, exploiters, careerists, and so on. They are confronted with situations in which the classic metaphors of herding cats and keeping butterflies in formation are all too real.

Ultimately, however, as the *Good to Great* books suggest, the minimalist approach to management may work best in the long run.[40] It eventually is more effective; producing more worker autonomy/satisfaction, which I have found generally is the most powerful motivator of all. The minimalist manager can focus on strategy, the big picture, long-term external relations where they can uniquely contribute. In the end, fewer managers are needed since, in effect, each worker becomes their own. Hopefully this discussion of a contrarian approach to management suggests some of the heuristic benefits to a dosage metaphor which allows us to consider the case for the smallest effective dose, or ultimately no dose at all.

In the end a metaphor works or it does not, its beauty is in the eye of the beholder. Hopefully I have demonstrated that the dosage metaphor has historically permeated organizational theory and that it is a strong metaphor that is markedly emphatic and resonant.[41] The study of dosage can be deep and rich, offering a myriad of possible approaches to specific problems that managers must confront every day.

Notes

Preface

1. Farace and Johnson (1974).
2. Johnson (2008).

Prologue

1. With the resulting meaning the "therapeutic agent."

Chapter 1

1. Zimmerman, Sypher, and Haas (1996).
2. Stafford (2005).
3. Afifi and Afifi (2009), p. 1.
4. Johnson (1996).
5. Cross, Nohria, and Parker (2004), p. 67.
6. Krackhardt (1994).
7. Hibbard and Peters (2003).
8. Surowiecki (2004).
9. Palmer and Dunford (1996).
10. Grant and Oswick (1996), p. 1.
11. However, the science of proteomics promises a new era of personalized medicine where our knowledge of genomics will allow us to much more power-
fully predict which agents will work for which people.

Chapter 2

1. Koch and Deetz (1981).
2. Grant and Oswick (1996), p. 1, italics in original.
3. Grant and Oswick (1996).
4. Cohen and March (1986).
5. Schon (1979).
6. Grant and Oswick (1996).

7. This playful experimentation is one of the more interesting aspects of meta-phor. All of us in applying concepts familiar to us to new terrain are often delighted with the results, but we are also aware that when we push things too far we run the risk of degenerating into increasingly silly arguments.

8. Petrie (1979).

9. Boxenbaum and Rouleau (2011); Cole and Leide (2006); Cornelissen (2006); Morgan (1986); Oswick, Fleming, and Hanlon (2011); and Palmer and Dunford (1996).

10. Krippendorf (1993); Littlejohn and Foss (2011).

11. Grant and Oswick (1996).

12. Grant and Oswick (1996).

13. Fligstein and Maradita (1992), p. 20 quoted in Swedberg (1994).

14. Slater (2004).

15. Slater (2004).

16. Sherif and Sherif (1964).

17. Lane, Koka, and Pathak (2006).

18. Cross et al. (2004), p. 51.

19. Gales, Porter, and Mansour-Cole (1992).

20. March (1991).

21. Hansen and Haas (2001).

22. Johnson, Andrews, Case, Allard, and Johnson (2006).

23. Goldsmith (2001).

24. Many communication activities follow a temporal patterning. So, for exam-ple, there are regular rhythms to use of social media with high levels of usage by college students starting midday Friday through midday Sunday and a weekday pattern at all other times (Golder, 2006). Similarly it has been sug-gested that the ordering of communication modalities has important conse-quences for the outcomes of performance appraisal interviews (Gordon and Miller, 2011).

25. Farace, Taylor, and Stewart (1978).

26. Kohane, Masys, and Altman (2006).

27. Katz and Kahn (1978).

28. Dearing, Meyer, and Kazmierczak (1994); Fidler and Johnson (1984).

29. Tushman (1978, 1979).

30. Kolb (1996).

31. Jablin (1978).

32. Morgan (1986).

33. Grant and Oswick (1996).

34. Mangham (1996).

35. Burns and Stalker (1961).

36. Koch and Deetz (1981).

37. Burns (1963, January 31); Burns and Stalker (1961).
38. Aldrich (2008).
39. One shortcoming of this view is that evolution takes a considerable amount of time to unfold. In our fast moving world this would often imply that certain species of organizations will die out. However, in their original conception Burns and Stalker (1961) saw organic forms of organization as more adaptable than mechanistic forms, because they did not rely on a preconceived plan and workers would be more free to respond to changing circumstances; Burns (Burns, 1963, January 31). Contemporary biomedical research is also demonstrating that there are times when the environment can even introduce dramatic changes in the genetic code.
40. Except in vestigial cases, like appendices, for which there is even recent research indicates something is lost.
41. Burns and Stalker (1961).
42. Burns and Stalker (1961).
43. Mangham (1996).
44. Mangham (1996).
45. Ritti (1986).
46. Morgan (1986).
47. Cohen, March, and Olson (1972).
48. Weick (1976).
49. Beninger (1986).
50. Koch and Deetz (1981).
51. Eisenberg (1990).
52. Putnam (1999).
53. Putnam (2006).
54. Putnam (2006).
55. Greenberg and Roseman (2003).
56. Fukami (1993).
57. Morgan (1986).
58. Burrell (1996).
59. Larwood (1992).
60. Cohen and March (1986).
61. In some ways this harkens back to Likert's (1967) linking pin notion.
62. Littlejohn and Foss (2011).
63. Putnam (1999); Putnam and Boys (2006).
64. Deetz (1986); Reddy (1979).
65. Putnam (1998, 1999); Putnam and Boys (2006).
66. Owen-Smith and Powell (2004).
67. Pacanowsky and O'Donnell-Trujillo (1982).

68. Indeed, a network program, PAJEK, is named for the Slovenian word for spider (2005).
69. Perhaps an indication that the medium really is the message. We will return to these issues when we discuss media richness in Chapter 3.
70. Cornelissen (2005); Palmer and Dunford (1996).
71. Cornellissen (2005).
72. Oswick and Jones (2006).
73. Cornelissen (2005); Cornelissen (2006).
74. Krippendorf (1993).
75. Grant and Oswick (1996); Deal and Kennedy (1982).
76. Smircich and Calas (1987).
77. Frost (1987).
78. Meyer (1984).
79. The process by which this is accomplished may relate directly to the concept of strategic ambiguity put forth by Eisenberg (1984). At its heart this concept refers to the intentional omission of contextual cues in messages to promote multiple interpretations of messages in receivers. Strategic ambiguity promotes the integration of diverse coalitions, facilitates organizational change, and preserves privileged positions.
80. Hiemstra (1983).
81. Grant and Oswick (1996).

Chapter 3

1. Lawrence and Lorsch (1967); Woodward (1965).
2. Downs, Clampitt, and Pfeiffer (1988).
3. Egelhoff (1982); Fry and Smith (1987).
4. Shaw (1971).
5. Fonner and Roloff (2010).
6. Woodward (1965).
7. Woodward (1965).
8. Woodward (1965).
9. Woodward (1965).
10. In addition, the most successful firms fell within these medians for their respective industries.
11. This highlights the importance of frequency and repetition of dosages, something that Gordon and Miller (2011) have stressed is critical to the success of performance appraisal systems.
12. Simpson (1952).
13. Randolph and Finch (1977).
14. Van de Ven, Delbecq, and Koenig (1976).

15. Lawrence and Lorsch (1967).
16. Galbraith (1995); Lawrence and Lorsch (1967).
17. March and Simon (1958), p. 162, italics in original.
18. Interestingly the development of these more specialized integrating mechanisms is viewed quite dramatically as a pathological response to changing environmental circumstances by Burns and Stalker (1961) whose work strongly influenced Lawrence and Lorsch's approach.
19. Lawrence and Lorsch (1967), p. 2, italics in original.
20. Cross, Nohria, and Parker (2004), p. 51.
21. Krackhardt (1994).
22. Hoopes and Postrel (1999).
23. Goldenson (1984), p. 137.
24. Rogers and Shoemaker (1971), p. 24.
25. Berlo (1960). p. 64.
26. Berlo (1960), p. 61.
27. Schramm (1973).
28. Schramm (1973).
29. Fulk and Boyd (1991); Johnson (1997); Markus (1994).
30. Rice (1993); Steinfeld, Jin, and Ku (1987).
31. Rogers (1962).
32. Rice and Associates (1984).
33. Wright (1999).
34. Durlak (1987).
35. Durlak (1987).
36. Short, Williams, and Christie (1976).
37. Walther (1994).
38. Ruchinskas (1983).
39. Sullivan (1995).
40. Fulk, Steinfield, Schmitz, and Power (1987); Steinfeld et al. (1987).
41. Fulk et al. (1987).
42. Daft and Macintosh (1981).
43. Hiemstra (1982); Picot, Klingenberg, and Kranzle (1982); Van de Ven (1976).
44. Daft and Lengel (1986); Lengel and Daft (1988).
45. Daft and Lengel (1986), p. 560.
46. Sitkin, Sutcliffe, and Barrios-Chaplin (1992).

Chapter 4

1. Knoke and Kuklinski (1982).
2. Katz and Kahn (1978).

3. Lincoln and McBride (1985).
4. Richards (1985).
5. Johnson and Smith (1985), sour/qhPen.
6. Unreciprocated linkages, linkages where one party does not agree that a relationship exists, are quite frequent in organizations (Monge, Edwards, & Kirste, 1978), for example, report percentages of reciprocation ranging from 37 to 100 percent across a number of empirical studies.
7. Ashford, Blatt, and VandeWalle (2003).
8. Miller and Jablin (1991).
9. Blau (1954).
10. Richards (1985).
11. Watts (2003).
12. Jablin (1980).
13. Eisenberg et al. (1985); Minor (1983).
14. Burt (1983), p. 37.
15. Minor (1983).
16. Hartman and Johnson (1989).
17. Hartman and Johnson (1989).
18. Granovetter (1973).
19. Friedkin (1980, 1982); Weimann (1983).
20. Granovetter (1982).
21. Albrecht and Adelman (1987).
22. Granovetter (1982).
23. Cook (1982); Hall (2003); partially because of their linkage to underlying economic theory.
24. Stafford (2005); Stafford and Canary (1991).
25. Bellah, Madsen, Sullivan, Swidler, and Tipton (1991).
26. Oxford English Dictionary (1989).
27. Eisenberg et al. (1985).
28. McGuiness (1991).
29. Von Hayek (1991).
30. Geertz (1973, 1978).
31. Lorenz (1991); Powell (1990).
32. Kirman (2001).
33. Jablin (1985); Downs et al. (1988).
34. Jablin (1979), p. 1202.
35. Jablin (1981).
36. Parks (1982).
37. Stafford (2003); Stafford and Canary (1991).

38. Afifi and Afifi (2009).
39. Bochner (1982), p. 120.
40. Littlejohn (1989).
41. Bochner (1982).
42. Parks (1982).
43. Parks (1982).
44. Bochner (1984).
45. Parks (1982).
46. Stafford (2003).
47. Jablin (1978).
48. Dansereau and Markham (1987).
49. Rogers (1987).
50. Jablin (1978).
51. Eisenberg and Whetten (1987).
52. Kanter (1977); Pfeffer (1982).
53. Jablin (1979).
54. Jablin (1978).
55. Jablin (1981).
56. Putnam (2000).
57. McPherson, Smith-Lovin, and Brashears (2006).
58. Altman and Taylor (1973).
59. Afifi and Afifi (2009).
60. Petronio (2002).
61. Petronio (2002).
62. Petronio and Reierson (2009).
63. Littlejohn and Foss (2011).
64. Marwell and Schmitt (1967).
65. Tannenbaum (1966).
66. Jablin (1979).
67. Blair, Roberts, and McKechnie (1985).
68. Hirokawa and Miyahara (1986).
69. Milardo (1983).
70. Granovetter (1973).
71. Pfeffer (1978).
72. Pelz (1952); Dansereau and Markham (1987).
73. Milardo (1983).
74. Parks and Adelman (1983); Parks, Stan, and Eggert (1983).
75. McPhee (1988).
76. Katz and Kahn (1978).

77. Katz and Kahn (1978).
78. Pelz (1952).
79. Dansereau and Markham (1987).

Chapter 5

1. Zimmerman et al. (1996), p. 200.
2. Downs et al. (1988); Provan and Milward (2001); This can be partially attributed to the general emphasis of the social sciences on psychological processes, such as attitude formation (1978, 1982). As a result, much less is known about people's actual behavior than about what they think they will do.
3. Downs et al. (1988), p. 173.
4. Farace and Johnson (1974).
5. Johnson (2005).
6. Cowan and Jonard (2009); Watts (2002); Similarly, in spite of popular hype, empirical work on Facebook found that messages were sent only infrequently, with an average of less than one message per user per week (Golder, 2006).
7. Rogers and Kincaid (1981); Valente (1995).
8. Fidler and Johnson (1984).
9. Monge and Miller (1988).
10. Gales et al. (1992).
11. Burt (1987).
12. Valente (1995).
13. Van de Ven et al. (1976).
14. Eisenberg (1990).
15. Menard (1991).
16. Bach (1989).
17. Valente (1995).
18. Johnson (2005).
19. Kolb (1996), p. 457, italics in original.
20. Robinson (2010).
21. Babrow and Matthais (2009).
22. Galbraith (1974).
23. Eppler and Mengis (2004).
24. Lawrence and Lorsch (1967).
25. Cross et al. (2004), p. 51.
26. Krackhardt (1994).
27. DeLuca and Atuahene-Gima (2007), p. 107.
28. Stohl and Redding (1987).

29. Daft and Huber (1987); O'Reilly and Pondy (1979).
30. Downs (1967).
31. Hansen (2002).
32. Bolton and Dewatripoint (1994).
33. Kilduff and Tsai (2003).
34. Hansen (2002).
35. Russo and Koesten (2005).
36. Balkundi and Harrison (2006).
37. Leavitt (1951).
38. Leavitt (1951); Shaw (1971).
39. Shaw (1971).
40. Guetskow and Simon (1955).
41. Katz and Kahn (1978).
42. Ahuja and Carley (1999); Krackhardt (1989).
43. Lee (2007), p. 22.
44. Kogut (2000), p. 408.
45. Zipf (1949).
46. Bates (2005); Case (2005); Hardy (1982). Shortly thereafter Wilbur Schramm (1954) developed a formula for determining which mass media offerings would be selected: the fraction of selection equaled the expectation of reward divided by the effort required.
47. Markey (2007); Somewhat relatedly, less than 20 percent of the general populace followed up on referrals by information specialists to professionals or institutions for answers to their questions (Chen and Hernon, 1982). Even when individuals need information they often do not actively, comprehensively search for it; rather they will wait until they accidentally stumble across the information, often in interpersonal encounters (Scott, 1991). "Many respondents reported that they made use of an information provider only as an afterthought in relation to another need" (Chen and Hernon, 1982, p. 57).
48. Hardy (1982); Rice and Shook (1990).
49. Case (2007); Johnson (1996).
50. Allen (1977); Blau (1954).
51. Allen (1977).
52. March (1994).
53. Case (2005); Johnson (1997); Johnson et al. (2006); However, there does appear to be an exception to this in the instance of communication stars. The communication stars explanation suggested that the two distinctive external and internal communication roles can be played by the same individual who is predisposed to high levels of communication (Aldrich & Herker, 1977; M. W. Allen, 1989; Friedman & Podolny, 1992; R. Katz & Tushman, 1981a, 1981b; Tushman & Scanlan, 1981b). While it would seem obvious

that there are finite limits to the amount of communication one can engage in (Baker, 1992), several empirical studies suggest that individuals who are high communicators in one setting are also high in others; that heavy users of one information medium related to work are likely to be users of other media that also carry this same information (Carroll & Teo, 1996; Paisley, 1980, 1993; Weedman, 1992), which is also a finding of more general media use studies (Berelson & Steiner, 1964).

54. Pirolli and Card (1999).
55. Lee (2007), p. 33.
56. March (1994); Farace, Monge, and Russell (1977).
57. Bates (2005); Pirolli and Card (1999).
58. In recent years communication research has shown a curious tendency to ignore fundamental issues critical to practice. This is certainly the case with productivity, effectiveness, and efficiency issues. One of the most basic reasons for exploring the comparison between dosage and communication is that by applying the dosage metaphor to communication theory and research we have a framework for understanding how far we need to go.
59. Daft and Lengel (1986).

Chapter 6

1. Armenikas and Bedeian (1992), p. 297.
2. Rogers (2003).
3. Rogers and Adhikayra (1979), p. 79.
4. Bennis (1965).
5. Reagans and McEvily (2003).
6. Farace et al. (1978).
7. Fidler and Johnson (1984).
8. Leonard-Barton and Deschamps (1988).
9. Fidler and Johnson (1984).
10. French and Raven (1959).
11. Johnson (1990).
12. Goldhar, Bragaw, and Schwartz (1976).
13. Fidler and Johnson (1984).
14. Galbraith (1982).
15. Huckfeldt, Johnson, and Sprague (2004).
16. Marshak (1996).
17. Leonard (2006).
18. Szulanski (1996, 2003).
19. Berlo (1960).

20. Hinds and Pfeffer (2003).
21. DeLuca and Atuahence-Gima (2007).
22. Gold, Malhotra, and Segars (2001).
23. Reddy (1979), p. 295.
24. Cohen and Levinthal (1989, 1994).
25. Jansen, Van Den Bosch, and Volberda (2005).
26. Uzzi and Spiro (2005).
27. Zahra and George (2002).
28. March (1991).
29. Taylor and Greve (2006).
30. March (1991), p. 76.
31. Taylor and Greve (2006).
32. Balkundi and Harrison (2006).
33. Uzzi and Spiro (2005).
34. Rowley, Behrens, and Krackhardt (2000).
35. Katila and Ahuja (2002).
36. Hansen (1999).
37. Ahuja (2000).
38. Mohrman, Tenkasi, and Mohrman (2003).
39. Kratzer, Leenders, and van Engelen (2004).
40. Kanter (1988).
41. Kratzer et al. (2004).
42. Kratzer et al. (2004).
43. Burt (2005).
44. Perry-Smith and Shalley (2003).
45. Uzzi and Spiro (2005).
46. Burt (1980).
47. Rogers (1995); Rogers and Kincaid (1981).
48. Burt (1987).
49. Burt (1982), p. 110.
50. Burt (1987); Burt and Dorien (1982); Burt and Uchiyama (1989); Friedkin (1984).
51. Burt and Doreian (1982), p. 112.
52. Hartman and Johnson (1989), p. 524.
53. Burt (1982, 1987).
54. McGrath and Krackhardt (2003).
55. Katz and Lazersfeld (1955).
56. Burt (1980).
57. Reagans and McEvily (2003).
58. Coleman, Katz, and Menzel (1957).
59. Van den Bulte and Lillien (2001).

60. Valente (2006).
61. McGrath and Krackhardt (2003).
62. Danes, Hunter, and Woelfel (1978); Goldberg (1954); Zimbardo (1960).
63. Fan (2002).
64. McGrath and Krackhardt (2003).
65. McGrath and Krackhardt (2003).
66. Danowski (1980).
67. Woelful, Cody, Gillham, and Holmes (1980).
68. Snyder and Hamilton (2002).
69. Huckfeldt et al. (2004).
70. Lawrence and Lorsch (1967).
71. Abelson (1964); French (1959); Huckfeldt et al. (2004).
72. Albrecht (1979).
73. Erickson (1982).
74. Monge and Contractor (2003).
75. Corman and Scott (1994); Kuhn and Corman (2003).
76. Kuhn and Corman (2003), p. 200, italics in original.
77. Kuhn and Corman (2003), p. 199.
78. Hartman and Johnson (1989), p. 525.
79. Burt (1982, 1987).
80. Hartman and Johnson (1989), p. 525.
81. Watts (2003).
82. Valente (1995).
83. Watts (2002).
84. Valente (1995).
85. Watts (2002).
86. Albrecht and Hall (1989); Kanter (1983).
87. Rice, Grant, Schmitz, and Torobin (1988).
88. Burt (2002).

Chapter 7

1. Choo and Auster (1993); Thomas, Clark, and Gioia (1993).
2. Emery and Trist (1965).
3. de Chardin (1961).
4. Weick (1969).
5. Contractor and Seibold (1993); Giddens (1991); Poole and McPhee (1983).
6. Dervin (1997).
7. Weick (1969).
8. Simon (1991).

9. Rowley et al. (2000).

10. Aldrich and Herker (1977).

11. Leifer and Delbecq (1978), pp. 40–41.

12. Adams (1976).

13. Johnson and Chang (2000).

14. Eisenberg et al. (1985), p. 240.

15. Friedman and Podolny (1992), p. 32.

16. Katz and Tushman (1981a); Tushman (1978, 1979).

17. Allen (1966).

18. Basu and Palazzo (2008).

19. Heider (1946).

20. Broom (1977); Grunig and Hunt (1984).

21. Clarkson (1995).

22. Grunig and Hunt (1984).

23. In spite of many consequent problems Johnson & Johnson has had with their products.

24. Covello (1992).

25. Classically advertising was the essential tool used to match the demands for an organization's products to its capacity to produce them, but a complete discussion of it is beyond the scope of this book.

26. Salmon and Atkin (2003).

27. Noar, Palmgreen, and Zimmerman (2009), p. 109.

28. Noar (2006).

29. Noar (2006).

30. Flora, Maccoby, and Farquhar (1989).

31. Flora et al. (1989), p. 250; Rimal, Flora, and Schooler (1999).

32. Noar (2006).

33. Schramm (1972).

34. Flay (1981); Robertson and Wortzel (1977).

35. Alcalay (1983); Katz and Lazarsfeld (1955); Lichter (1987); Roger and Storey (1987).

36. Lichter (1987).

37. Alcalay (1983).

38. Hyman and Sheatsley (1947); Real (2008).

39. Cialdini (2001).

40. Freimuth, Stein, and Kean (1989).

41. Morgan, King, and Ivie (2011).

42 McGuire (1989).

43. Noar (2006).

44. Snyder and Hamilton (2002).

45. Lichtenstein and Glasgow (1992)

46. Hornik (2002).
47. Siegel and Biener (2002).
48. Dijkstra, Buijtels, and Van Raaij (2005); Lichtenstein and Glasgow (1992).
49. Real (2008).
50. Lichtenstein and Glasgow (1992).
51. Snyder and Hamilton (2002), p. 360.
52. Salmon and Atkin (2003), p. 467.
53. Palmgreen, Donohew, Lorch, Hoyle, and Stephenson (2002).
54. Salmon and Atkin (2003).
55. Salmon and Atkin (2003).
56. Snyder and Hamilton (2002).

Chapter 8

1. Mukherjee (2010), p. 143.
2. The issue of amount and frequency in terms of building up to a certain level of critical mass have been rigorously detailed in some network analysis approaches.
3. Rogers (2003).
4. Putnam and Boys (2006).
5. We do not have Darwinian approaches to old ideas which all still may be in place somewhere. In other words, do we have any mechanism for eliminating the old? Just as physicians seldom learn new tricks once they leave school, in spite of licensing that depends on continuing education, there are many professors who teach for a generation without ever assimilating the new.
6. Marshak (1996).
7. Mangham (1996).
8. Oswick and Grant (1996).
9. Tsoukas (1991).
10. In their highly influential study of university presidents Cohen and March (1986) suggest that one basic problem for universities, and for their leaders, is a failure to identify a satisfactory metaphor for how they function.
11. Atkin (1981), p. 47.
12. Johnson and Case (in press).
13. Reddy (1979).
14. Dervin (1980).
15. Hall (1981); Rowley and Turner (1978).
16. Morley (1993).
17. Katz, Blumler, and Gurevitch (1974).
18. Dervin (1980).
19. Katz (1968).

20. Drucker (1974).
21. March and Simon (1958).
22. Fonner and Roloff (2010).
23. Hansen and Haas (2001).
24. Glasgow, Klesges, Dzewaltowski, Bull, and Estabrooks (2004).
25. Rogers (2003).
26. Pirolli and Card (1999); Simon (1987); Van de Ven (1986).
27. Fortner (1995).
28. Drucker (Drucker, 1988).
29. Aldrich and Ruef (2006).
30. Baldridge (1971), p. 207.
31. Aldrich and Ruef (2006).
32. As do helicopter managers that do not let their worker grow through failure and experimentation.
33. Kellerman (2008).
34. Watts (2003).
35. Zaltman (1994).
36. Argote (1999); Argote and Epple (1990); Govindarajan and Trimble (2005).
37. Collins (2001).
38. March and Simon (1958).
39. Ehrenberg (2002), p. 14.
40. Collins (2001).
41. Black (1979).

References

Abelson, R. P. (1964). Mathematical models of the distribution of attitudes under controversy. In N. Frederiksen & H. Gulliksen (Eds.), *Contributions to mathematical psychology*. New York: Holt, Rinehart and Winston.

Adams, J. S. (1976). The structure and dynamics of behavior in organizational boundary roles. In M. D. Dunnette (Ed.), *Handbook of industrial and organizational psychology* (pp. 1175–1199). Chicago, IL: Rand McNally.

Afifi, T. D., & Afifi, W. A. (2009). Introduction. In T. D. Afifi & W. A. Afifi (Eds.), *Uncertainty, information management, and disclosure decisions: Theories and applications* (pp. 1–5). New York: Routledge.

Ahuja, G. (2000). Collaboration networks, structural holes, and innovation: A longitudinal study. *Administrative Science Quarterly, 45*, 425–455.

Ahuja, M. K., & Carley, K. M. (1999). Network structure in virtual organizations. *Organization Science, 10*, 741–757.

Albrecht, T. L. (1979). The role of communication in perceptions of organizational climate. In D. Nimmo (Ed.), *Communication Yearbook 3* (pp. 343–357). New Brunswick, NJ: Transaction Books.

Albrecht, T. L., & Adelman, M. B. (1987). Rethinking the relationship between communication and social support: An introduction. In T. L. Albrecht & M. B. Adelman (Eds.), *Communicating social support* (pp. 13–16). Newbury Park, CA: Sage.

Albrecht, T. L., & Hall, B. (1989). *Relational and content differences between elites and outsiders in innovation networks*. Paper presented at the Annual Meetings of the International Communication Association Convention, San Francisco, CA.

Alcalay, R. (1983). The impact of mass communication campaigns in the health field. *Social Science and Medicine, 17*, 87–94.

Aldrich, H. E., (2008). *Organizations and environments*. Stanford, CA: Stanford Business Books.

Aldrich, H. E., & Herker, D. (1977). Boundary spanning roles and organizational structure. *Academy of Management Review, 2*, 217–230.

Aldrich, H. E., & Ruef, M. (2006). *Organizations evolving* (2nd ed.). Thousand Oaks, CA: Sage.

Allen, M. W. (1989). *Factors influencing the power of a linking role: An investigation into interorganizational boundary spanning*. Doctoral Dissertation. Louisiana State University. Baton Rouge, LA.

Allen, T. J. (1966). Performance of information channels in the transfer of technology. *Industrial Management Review, 8*, 87–98.

Allen, T. J. (1977). *Managing the flow of technology: Technology transfer and the dissemination of technological information within the R&D organization.* Cambridge, MA: MIT Press.

Altman, I., & Taylor, D. A. (1973). *Social penetration: The development of interpersonal relationships.* New York: Holt, Rinehart and Winston.

Argote, L. (1999). *Organizational learning: Creating, retaining and transferring knowledge.* Boston, MA: Kluwer Academic Publishers.

Argote, L., & Epple, D. (1990). Learning curves in manufacturing. *Science, 247,* 920–924.

Armenakis, A. A., & Bedeian, A. G. (1992). The role of metaphors in organizational change: Change agent and change target perspectives. *Group and Organization Management, 17,* 242–248.

Ashford, S. J., Blatt, R., & VandeWalle, D. (2003). Reflections on the looking glass: A review of research on feedback seeking behavior in organizations. *Journal of Management, 29,* 773–799.

Atkin, C. K. (1981). Mass communication research principles for health education. In M. Meyer (Ed.), *Health education by television and radio: Contributions to an international conference with a selected bibliography* (pp. 41–55). New York: K. G. Saur.

Babrow, A. S., & Matthias, M. S. (2009). Generally unseen challenges in uncertainty management: An application of problematic integration theory. In T. D. Afifi & W. A. Afifi (Eds.), *Uncertainty, information management, and disclosure decisions: Theories and applications* (pp. 9–25). New York: Routledge.

Bach, B. (1989). The effect of multiplex relationships upon innovation adoption: A reconsideration of Rogers' model. *Communication monographs, 56,* 133–150.

Baker, W. E. (1992). Network organization in theory and practice. In N. Nohria & R. G. Eccles (Eds.), *Networks and organizations: Structure, form, and action* (pp. 397–429). Boston, MA: Harvard Business School Press.

Baldridge, J. V. (1971). *Power and conflict in the university: Research in the sociology of complex organizations.* New York: John Wiley.

Balkundi, P., & Harrison, D. A. (2006). Ties, leaders, and time in teams: Strong inference about network structure's effect on team viability and performance. *Academy of Management Journal, 49,* 49–68.

Basu, K., & Palazzo, G. (2008). Corporate social responsibility: A process model of sensemaking. *Academy of Management Review, 33*(1), 122–136.

Bates, M. J. (2005). An introduction to metatheories, theories, and models. In K. E. Fisher, S. Erdelez, & L. McKechnie (Eds.), *Theories of information behavior* (pp. 1–24). Medford, NJ: Information Today.

Bellah, R. N., Madsen, R., Sullivan, W. M., Swidler, A., & Tipton, S. M. (1991). *The good society.* New York: Knopf.

Beninger, J. R. (1986). *The control revolution: Technological and economic origins of the information society.* Cambridge, MA: Harvard University Press.

Bennis, W. G. (1965). Theory and method in applying behavioral science to planned organizational change. *Applied Behavioral Science, 1*, 337–360.

Berelson, B., & Steiner, G. A. (1964). *Human behavior: An inventory of scientific findings.* New York: Harcourt, Brace & World.

Berlo, D. K. (1960). *The process of communication: An introduction to theory and practice.* New York: Holt, Rinehart and Winston.

Black, M. (1979). More about metaphor. In A. Ortony (Ed.), *Metaphor and thought* (pp. 19–43). Cambridge, UK: Cambridge University Press.

Blair, R., Roberts, K. H., & McKechnie, P. (1985). Vertical and network communication in organizations: The present and the future. In R. D. McPhee & P. K. Tompkins (Eds.), *Organizational communication: Traditional themes and new directions* (pp. 55–78). Beverly Hills, CA: Sage.

Blau, P. M. (1954). Patterns of interaction among a group of officials in a government agency. *Human Relations, 7*, 337–348.

Bochner, A. P. (1982). On the efficacy of openness in close relationships. In M. Burgoon (Ed.), *Communication Yearbook 5* (pp. 109–144). New Brunswick, NJ: Transaction Books.

Bochner, A. P. (1984). The functions of human communication in interpersonal bonding. In C. C. Arnold & J. W. Bowers (Eds.), *Handbook of rhetorical and communication theory* (pp. 554–621). Boston, MA: Allyn and Bacon.

Bolton, P., & Dewatripoint, M. (1994). The firm as a communication network. *Quarterly Journal of Economics, CIX*, 809–839.

Boxenbaum, E., & Rouleau, L. (2011). New knowledge products as a bicolage: Metaphors and scripts in organizational theory. *Academy of Management Review, 36*(2), 272–296.

Broom, G. M. (1977). Coorientational measurement of public issues. *Public Relations Review, 3*, 110–118.

Burns, T. (1963, January 31). Industry in a new age. *New Society, 1*, 17–20.

Burns, T., & Stalker, G. M. (1961). *The management of innovations.* London: Tavistock publications.

Burrell, G. (1996). Normal science, paradigms, metaphors, discourses and geneologies of analysis. In S. R. Clegg, C. Hardy, & W. R. Nord (Eds.), *Handbook of organization studies* (pp. 642–658). London: Sage.

Burt, R. S. (1980). Innovation as a structural interest: Rethinking the impact of network position of innovation ddoption. *Social Networks, 2*, 327–355.

Burt, R. S. (1982). *Toward a structural theory of action: Network models of social structure, perception, and action.* New York: Academic Press.

Burt, R. S. (1983). A note on inference concerning network subgroups. In R. S. Burt & M. J. Minor (Eds.), *Applied network analysis: A methodological introduction* (pp. 283–301). Beverly Hills, CA: Sage.

Burt, R. S. (1987). Social contagion and innovation: Cohesion versus structural equivalence. *Applied Journal of Psychology, 92*, 1287–1335.

Burt, R. S. (2002). Bridge decay. *Social Networks, 24*, 333–363.

Burt, R. S. (2005). *Brokerage and closure: An introduction to social capital.* New York: Oxford University Press.

Burt, R. S., & Doreian, P. (1982). Testing a structural model of perception: Conformity and deviance with respect to journal norms in elite sociological methodology. *Quality and Quantity, 16*, 109–150.

Burt, R. S., & Uchiyama, T. (1989). The conditional significance of communication for interpersonal influence. In M. Kochen (Ed.), *The small world.* Norwood, NJ: Ablex.

Carroll, G. R., & Teo, A. C. (1996). On the social networks of managers. *Academy of Management Journal, 39*, 421–440.

Case, D. O. (2005). Principle of least effort. In K. E. Fisher, S. Erdelez, & L. McKechnie (Eds.), *Theories of information behavior* (pp. 289–292). Medford, NJ: Information Today.

Case, D. O. (2007). *Looking for information* (2nd ed.). Bingley, UK: Emerald Group Publishing.

Chen, C., & Hernon, P. (1982). *Information seeking: Assessing and anticipating user needs.* New York: Neal-Schuman Publishers.

Choo, C. W., & Auster, E. (1993). Environmental scanning: Acquisition and use of information by managers. *Annual review of information science and technology* (Vol. 28, pp. 279–314). Medford, NJ: Learned Information.

Cialdini, R. B. (2001). *Influence: Science and practice* (4th ed.). Boston, MA: Allyn and Bacon.

Clarkson, M. B. E. (1995). A stakeholder framework for analyzing and evaluating corporate social performance. *Academy of Management Review, 20*(1), 92–117.

Cohen, M. D., & March, J. G. (1986). *Leadership and ambiguity: The American college president* (2nd ed.). Boston, MA: Harvard Business School.

Cohen, M. D., March, J. G., & Olson, J. P. (1972). A garbage can model of organizational choice. *Administrative Science Quarterly, 17*, 1–25.

Cohen, W. M., & Levinthal, D. A. (1989). Innovation and learning: The two faces of R & D. *The Economic Journal, 99*, 569–596.

Cohen, W. M., & Levinthal, D. A. (1994). Fortune favors the prepared firm. *Management Science, 40*, 227–251.

Cole, C., & Leide, J. E. (2006). A cognitive framework for human information behavior: The place of metaphor in human information organizing behavior. In A. Spink & C. Cole (Eds.), *New direction in human information behavior* (pp. 171–202). The Netherlands: Springer.

Coleman, J., Katz, E., & Menzel, H. (1957). The diffusion of an innovation among physicians. *Sociometry, 20*, 253–270.

Collins, J. (2001). *Good to great: Why some companies make the leap ... and others don't.* New York: Harper Collins.

Contractor, N. S., & Seibold, D. R. (1993). Theoretical frameworks for the study of structuring process in group decision support systems: Adaptive structuration theory and self-organizing system theory. *Human Communication Research, 19*, 528–563.

Cook, K. S. (1982). Network structures from an exchange perspective. In P. V. Marsden & N. Lin (Eds.), *Social structure and network analysis* (pp. 177–199). Beverly Hills, CA: Sage.

Corman, S. R., & Scott, C. R. (1994). Perceived networks, activity foci, and observable communication in social collectives. *Communication Theory, 4*, 171–190.

Cornelissen, J. P. (2005). Beyond compare: Metaphor in organization theory. *Academy of Management Review, 30*, 751–764.

Cornelissen, J. P. (2006). Metaphor in organization theory: Progress and the past. *Academy of Management Review, 31*, 485–488.

Covello, V. T. (1992). Risk communication: An emerging area of health communication research. In S. A. Deetz (Ed.), *Communication Yearbook 15* (pp. 359–372). Newbury Park, CA: Sage.

Cowan, R., & Jonard, N. (2009). Knowledge portfolios and the organization of innovation networks. *Academy of Management Review, 34*(2), 320–342.

Cross, R., Nohria, N., & Parker, A. (2004). Six myths about informal networks-and how to overcome them. In E. Lesser & L. Prusak (Eds.), *Creating value with knowledge: Insights from the IBM Institute for Business Value* (pp. 47–60). New York: Oxford University Press.

Cross, R., Parker, A., Prusak, L., & Borgatti, S. P. (2004). Knowing what we know: Supporting knowledge creation and sharing in social networks. In E. Lesser & L. Prusak (Eds.), *Creating value with knowledge: Insights from the IBM Institute for Business Value* (pp. 61–81). New York: Oxford University Press.

Daft, R. L., & Huber, G. P. (1987). How organizations learn: A communication framework. In N. D. Tomoso & S. B. Bacharach (Eds.), *Research in organizational behavior* (pp. 1–36). Greenwich, CT: JAI Press.

Daft, R. L., & Lengel, R. H. (1986). Organizational information requirements: Media richness and structural design. *Management Science, 32*, 554–571.

Daft, R. L., & Macintosh, N. B. (1981). A tentative exploration into the amount and equivocality of information processing in organizational work units. *Administrative Science Quarterly, 26*, 207–224.

Danes, J. E., Hunter, J. E., & Woelfel, J. (1978). Mass communication and belief change: A test of three mathematical models. *Human Communication Research, 4*, 243–252.

Danowski, J. A. (1980). Group attitude uniformity and connectivity of organizational communication networks for production, innovation, maintenance content. *Human Communication Research, 6*, 299–308.

Dansereau, F., & Markham, S. E. (1987). The superior subordinate communication: Multiple levels of analysis. In F. M. Jablin, L. L. Putnam, K. H. Roberts, & L. W. Porter (Eds.), *Handbook of organizational communication: An interdisciplinary perspective* (pp. 343–388). Newbury Park, CA: Sage.

de Chardin, P. (1961). *The phenomenon of man*. New York: Harper.

de Nooy, W., Mrvar, A., & Batagelj, V. (2005). *Exploratory social network analysis with Pajek*. Cambridge: Cambridge University Press.

Deal, T., & Kennedy, A. (1982). *Corporate cultures*. Reading, MA: Addison-Wesley.

Dearing, J. W., Meyer, G., & Kazmierczak, J. (1994). Portraying the new: Communication between university innovators and potential users. *Science Communication, 16*, 11–42.

Deetz, S. (1986). Metaphors and the discursive production and reproduction of organization. In L. Thayer (Ed.), *Organization–Communication* (pp. 168–182). Norwood, NJ: Ablex.

DeLuca, L. M., & Atuahene-Gima, K. (2007). Market knowledge dimensions and cross-functional collaboration: Examining the different routes to product innovation performance. *Journal of Marketing, 71*, 95–112.

Dervin, B. (1980). Communication gaps and inequities: Moving toward a reconceptualization. In B. Dervin & M. J. Voight (Eds.), *Progress in communication sciences* (pp. 74–112). Norwood, NJ: Ablex.

Dervin, B. (1997). Given a context by any other name: Methodological tools for taming the unruly beast. In P. Vakkari, R. Savolainen & B. Dervin (Eds.), *Information seeking in context* (pp. 13–38). London: Taylor Graham.

Dijkstra, M., Buijtels, H. J. J. M., & VanRaaij, W. F. (2005). Separate and joint effects of medium type on consumer responses: A comparison of television, print, and the Internet. *Journal of Business Research, 58*, 377–386.

Downs, A. (1967). *Inside bureaucracy*. Boston, MA: Little, Brown.

Downs, C. W., Clampitt, P. G., & Pfeiffer, A. L. (1988). Communication and organizational outcomes. In G. M. Goldhaber & G. A. Barnett (Eds.), *Handbook of organizational communication* (pp. 171–212). Norwood, NJ: Ablex.

Drucker, P. F. (1974). *Management—Tasks, responsibilities, practices*. New York: Harper and Row.

Drucker, P. F. (1988). The coming of the new organization. *Harvard Business Review, 66*, 45–53.

Durlak, J. T. (1987). A typology of interactive media. In M. L. McLaughlin (Ed.), *Communication Yearbook 10* (pp. 743–757). Beverly Hills, CA: Sage.

Egelhoff, W. G. (1982). Strategy and structure in multinational corporations: An information processing approach. *Administrative Science Quarterly, 27*, 435–458.

Ehrenberg, R. G. (2002). *Tuition rising: Why college costs so much*. Cambridge, MA: Harvard University press.

Eisenberg, E. M. (1984). Ambiguity as strategy in organizational communication. *Communication Monographs, 51*, 277–242.

Eisenberg, E. M. (1990). Jamming: Transcendence through organizing. *Communication Research, 17*, 139–164.

Eisenberg, E. M., Farace, R. V., Monge, P. R., Bettinghaus, E. P., Kurchner Hawkins, R., Miller, K. I., et al. (1985). Communication linkages in interorganizational systems: Review and synthesis. In B. Dervin & M. Voight (Eds.), *Progress in communication sciences* (Vol. 6, pp. 231–261). New York: Ablex.

Eisenberg, E. M., & Whetten, M. G. (1987). Reconsidering openness in organizational communication. *Academy of Management Review, 12*, 418–426.

Emery, F., & Trist, E. (1965). The causal texture of organizational environment. *Human Relations, 18*, 21–32.

Eppler, M. J., & Mengis, J. (2004). The concept of information overload: A review of literature from organization science, accounting, marketing, MIS, and related disciplines. *The Information Society, 20*, 325–344.

Erickson, B. H. (1982). Networks, ideologies, and belief systems. In P. V. Marsden & N. Lin (Eds.), *Social structure and network analysis*. Beverly Hills, CA: Sage.

Fan, D. P. (2002). Impact of persuasive information on secular trends and health-related behaviors. In R. C. Hornik (Ed.), *Public health communication: Evidence for behavior change* (pp. 251–264). Mahwah, NJ: Lawrence Erlbaum Associates.

Farace, R. V., & Johnson, J. D. (1974). *Comparative analysis of human communication networks in selected formal organizations*. Paper presented at the International Communication Association Annual Convention, New Orleans, LA.

Farace, R. V., Monge, P. R., & Russell, H. (1977). *Communicating and organizing*. Reading, MA: Addison-Wesley.

Farace, R. V., Taylor, J. A., & Stewart, J. P. (1978). Criteria for evaluation of organizational communication effectiveness: Review and synthesis. In D. Nimmo (Ed.), *Communication Yearbook 2* (pp. 271–292). New Brunswick, NJ: Transaction Books.

Fidler, L. A., & Johnson, J. D. (1984). Communication and innovation implementation. *Academy of Management Review, 9*, 704–711.

Flay, B. R. (1981). On improving the chances of mass media health promotion programs causing meaningful changes in behavior. In M. Meyer (Ed.), *Health communication by television and radio* (pp. 56–91). New York: K. G. Sauer.

Flora, J. A., Maccoby, N., & Farquhar, J. W. (1989). Communication campaigns to prevent cardiovascular disease: The Stanford Community Studies.

In R. E. Rice & C. K. Atkin (Eds.), *Public communication campaigns* (2nd ed., pp. 233–252). Newbury Park, CA: Sage.

Fonner, K. L., & Roloff, M. E. (2010). Why teleworkers are more satisfied with their jobs than are office-based workers: When less contact is beneficial. *Journal of Applied Communication Research, 38*(4), 336–361.

Fortner, R. S. (1995). Excommunication in the information society. *Critical Studies in Mass Communication, 12*, 133–154.

Freimuth, V. S., Stein, J. A., & Kean, T. J. (1989). *Searching for health information: The Cancer Information Service model*. Philadelphia, PA: University of Pennsylvania Press.

French, J. R. P., Jr., & Raven, B. (1959). The bases of social power. In D. Cartwright (Ed.), *Studies in social power* (pp. 150–167). Ann Arbor, MI: Institute for Social Research.

Friedkin, N. E. (1980). A test of structural features of Granovetter's strength of weak ties theory. *Social Networks, 2*, 411–422.

Friedkin, N. E. (1982). Information flow through strong and weak ties in intraorganizational social networks. *Social Networks, 3*, 273–285.

Friedkin, N. E. (1984). Structural cohesion and equivalence: Explanation of social homogeneity. *Sociological Method and Research, 12*, 235–261.

Friedman, R. A., & Podolny, J. (1992). Differentiation of boundary spanning roles: Labor negotiations and implications for role conflict. *Administrative Science Quarterly, 37*, 28–47.

Frost, P. J. (1987). Power, politics, and influence. In F. M. Jablin, L. L. Putnam, K. H. Roberts, & L. W. Porter (Eds.), *Handbook of organizational communication: An interdisciplinary perspective* (pp. 503–548). Newbury Park, CA: Sage.

Fry, L. W., & Smith, D. A. (1987). Congruence, contingency, and theory building. *Academy of Management Review, 12*, 117–132.

Fukami, C. V. (1993). On being an irrational manager, or the art of herding cats. *Journal Management Inquiry, 2*, 306–307.

Fulk, J., & Boyd, B. (1991). Emerging theories of communication in organizations. *Journal of Management, 17*, 407–446.

Fulk, J., Steinfield, C. W., Schmitz, J., & Power, J. G. (1987). A social information proceessing model of media use in organizations. *Communication Research, 14*, 529–552.

Galbraith, J. R. (1974). Organizational design: An information processing view. *Interfaces, 4*, 28–36.

Galbraith, J. R. (1982). Designing the innovating organization. *Organizational Dynamics, 10*, 5–25.

Galbraith, J. R. (1995). *Designing organizations: An executive briefing on strategy, structure, and process*. San Francisco, CA: Jossey-Bass.

Gales, L., Porter, P., & Mansour-Cole, D. (1992). Innovation project technology, information processing and performance: A test of the Daft and Lengel conceptualization. *Journal of Engineering and Technology Management, 9*, 303–338.

Geertz, C. (1973). *The interpretation of cultures*. New York: Basic Books.

Geertz, C. (1978). The bazaar economy: Information and search in peasant marketing. *American Economic Review, 68*, 28–37.

Giddens, A. (1991). Structuration theory: Past, present and future. In C. G. A. Bryant & D. Jary (Eds.), *Gidden's theory of structuration: A critical appreciation* (pp. 201–221). New York: Routledge.

Glasgow, R. E., Klesges, L. M., Dzewaltowski, D. A., Bull, S. S., & Estabrooks, P. (2004). The future of health behavior change research: What is needed to improve translation of research into health promotion practice. *Annals of Behavioral Medicine, 27*, 3–12.

Gold, A. H., Malhotra, A., & Segars, A. H. (2001). Knowledge management: An organizational capabilities perspective. *Journal of Management Information Systems, 18*(1), 185–214.

Goldberg, S. C. (1954). Three situational determinants of conformity to social norms. *Journal of Abnormal and Social Psychology, 9*, 449–459.

Goldenson, R. M. (1984). *Longman dictionary of psychology and psychiatry*. New York: Longman.

Golder, S., Wilkinson, D., & Huberman, B. (2006). Rhythms of social interaction: Messaging within a massive online network. Palo Alto, CA: HP Labs.

Goldhar, J. D., Bragaw, L. W., & Schwartz, J. J. (1976). Information flows, management styles, and technological innovation. *IEEE Transactions on Engineering Management, , 23*, 51–62.

Goldsmith, D. (2001). A normative approach to the study of uncertainty and communication. *Journal of Communication, 51*(3), 514–533.

Gordon, M. E., & Miller, V. D. (2011). *Conversations about job performance: A communication perspective on the appraisal process*. New York: Business Expert Press.

Govindarajan, V., & Trimble, C. (2005). Organizational DNA for strategic innovation. *California Management Review, 47*, 47–76.

Granovetter, M. S. (1973). The strength of weak ties. *American Journal of Sociology, 78*, 1360–1380.

Granovetter, M. S. (1982). The strength of weak ties: A network theory revisited. In P. V. Marsden & N. Lin (Eds.), *Social structure in network analysis* (pp. 105–130). Beverly Hills, CA: Sage.

Grant, D., & Oswick, C. (1996). Introduction: Getting the measure of metaphors. In D. Grant & C. Oswick (Eds.), *Metaphor and organizations* (pp. 1–20). Thousand Oaks, CA: Sage.

Greenberg, S., & Roseman, M. (2003). Using a room metaphor to ease transitions in groupware. In M. S. Ackerman, V. Pipek, & V. Wulf (Eds.), *Sharing expertise: Beyond knowledge management.* Cambridge, MA: MIT Press.

Grunig, J. E., & Hunt, T. (1984). *Managing public relations.* New York: International Thomas Publishing.

Guetskow, H., & Simon, H. A. (1955). The impact of certain communication nets upon organization and performance in task oriented groups. *Management Science, 1,* 233–250.

Hall, H. J. (2003). Borrowed theory: Applying exchange theories in information science research. *Library and Information Science Research, 25,* 287–306.

Hall, H. J. (1981). Patterns in the use of information: The right to be different. *Journal of American Society for Information Science, 32,* 103–112.

Hansen, M. T. (1999). The search-transfer problem: The role of weak ties in sharing knowledge across organization subunits. *Administrative Science Quarterly, 44,* 82–111.

Hansen, M. T. (2002). Knowledge networks: Explaining effective knowledge sharing in multiunit companies. *Organization Science, 13,* 232–248.

Hansen, M. T., & Haas, M. R. (2001). Competing for attention in knowledge markets: Electronic document dissemination in a management consulting company. *Administrative Science Quarterly, 46,* 1–28.

Hardy, A. (1982). The selection of channels when seeking information: Cost/benefit vs least-effort. *Information Processing and Management, 18*(6), 289–293.

Hartman, R. L., & Johnson, J. D. (1989). Social contagion and multiplexity: Communication networks as predictors of commitment and role ambiguity. *Human Communication Research, 15,* 523–548.

Heider, F. (1946). Attitudes and cognitive organization. *Journal of Psychology, 21,* 107–112.

Hibbard, J. H., & Peters, E. (2003). Supporting informed consumer health care decisions: Data presentation approaches that facilitate the use of information in choice. *Annual Review of Public Health, 24,* 413–433.

Hiemstra, G. (1982). Telephone conferencing, concern for face, and organizational culture. In M. Burgoon (Ed.), *Communication Yearbook 6* (pp. 874–904). Beverly Hills, CA: Sage.

Hiemstra, G. (1983). You say you want a revolution? "Information technology" in organizations. In R. N. Bostrom (Ed.), *Communication Yearbook 7* (pp. 802–827). Beverly Hills, CA: Sage.

Hinds, P. J., & Pfeffer, J. (2003). Why organizations don't "know what they know" cognitive and motivational factors affecting the transfer of expertise. In M. S. Ackerman, V. Pipek & V. Wulf (Eds.), *Sharing expertise: Beyond knowledge management* (pp. 3–26). Cambridge, MA: MIT Press.

Hirokawa, R. Y., & Miyahara, R. K. (1986). *A comparison of influence strategies utilized by managers in American and Japanese organizations.* Paper presented at the International Communication Association, Chicago, IL.

Hoopes, D. G., & Postrel, S. (1999). Shared knowledge, "glitches," and product development performance. *Strategic Management Journal, 20,* 837.

Hornik, R. C. (2002). Epilogue: Evaluation design for public health communication programs. In R. C. Hornik (Ed.), *Public health communication: Evidence for behavior change* (pp. 385–405). Mahwah, NJ: Lawrence Erlbaum Associates.

Huckfeldt, R., Johnson, P. E., & Sprague, J. (2004). *Political disagreement: The survival of diverse opinions within communication networks.* New York: Cambridge University Press.

Hyman, H. H., & Sheatsley, P. B. (1947). Some reasons why information campaigns fail. *Public Opinion Quarterly, 11,* 412–423.

Jablin, F. M. (1978). Message response and "openness" in suprerior-subordinate communication. In B. D. Ruben (Ed.), *Communication Yearbook 2* (pp. 293–309). New Brunswick, NJ: Transaction Books.

Jablin, F. M. (1979). Superior-subordinate communication: The state-of-the-art. *Psychological Bulletin, 86,* 1201–1222.

Jablin, F. M. (1980). Organizational communication theory and research: An overview of communication climate and network research. In D. Nimmo (Ed.), *Communication Yearbook 4* (pp. 327–347). New Brunswick, NJ: Transaction Books.

Jablin, F. M. (1981). An exploratory study of subordinates perceptions of supervisory politics. *Communication Quarterly, 28,* 269–275.

Jablin, F. M. (1985). Taks/work relationships: A life-span perspective. In G. R. Miller & M. L. Knapp (Eds.), *Handbook of interpersonal communication* (pp. 615–654). Beverly Hills, CA: Sage.

Jansen, J. J. P., Van Den Bosch, F. A. J., & Volberda, H. W. (2005). Managing potential and realized absorptive capacity: How do organizational antecedents matter? *Academy of Management Journal, 48*(6), 999–1017.

Johnson, J. D. (1990). Effects of communicative factors on participation in innovations. *Journal of Business Communication, 27,* 7–24.

Johnson, J. D. (1996). *Information seeking: An organizational dilemma.* Westport, CT: Quorom Books.

Johnson, J. D. (1997). *Cancer-related information seeking.* Cresskill, NJ: Hampton Press.

Johnson, J. D. (2005). *Innovation and knowledge management: The Cancer Information Services Research Consortium.* Cheltenham, UK: Edward Elgar.

Johnson, J. D. (2008). Dosage: A bridging metaphor for theory and practice. *International Journal of Strategic Communication, 2,* 137–153.

Johnson, J. D., Andrews, J. E., Case, D. O., Allard, S. L., & Johnson, N. E. (2006). Fields and/or pathways: Contrasting and/or complementary views of information seeking. *Information Processing and Management, 42,* 569–582.

Johnson, J. D., & Case, D. O. (2012). *Health information seeking.* New York: Peter Lang.

Johnson, J. D., & Chang, H. J. (2000). Internal and external communication, boundary spanning, innovation adoption: An over-time comparison of three explanations of internal and external innovation communication in new organization form. *Journal of Business Communication, 37,* 238–263.

Johnson, J. D., & Smith, D. A. (1985). Effects of work dependency, response satisfaction and proximity on communication frequency. *Western Journal of Speech Communication, 49,* 217–231.

Kanter, R. M. (1977). *Men and women of the corporation.* New York: Basic Books.

Kanter, R. M. (1983). *The change masters: Innovation and entrepreneurship in the American corporation.* New York: Simon & Schuster.

Kanter, R. M. (1988). When a thousand flowers bloom: Structural, collective, and social conditions for innovations in organizations. *Research in Organizational Behavior, 10,* 169–211.

Katila, R., & Ahuja, G. (2002). Something old, something new: A longitudinal study of search behavior and new product introduction. *Academy of Management Journal, 45,* 1183–1194.

Katz, D., & Kahn, R. L. (1978). *The social psychology of organizations* (2nd ed.). New York: Wiley.

Katz, E. (1968). On reopening the question of selectivity in exposure to mass communications. In R. P. Abelson (Ed.), *Theories of cognitive consistency* (pp. 788–796). New York: Rand McNally.

Katz, E., Blumler, J. G., & Gurevitch, M. (1974). Uses of mass communication by the individual. In W. P. Davison (Ed.), *Mass communication research: Major issues and future directions* (pp. 11–35). New York: Praeger.

Katz, E., & Lazersfeld, P. F. (1955). *Personal influence: The part played by people in the flow of mass communications.* New York: The Free Press.

Katz, R., & Tushman, M. L. (1981). An investigation into the managerial roles and career paths of gatekeepers and project supervisors in a major R&D facility. *R&D Management, 11,* 103–110.

Kellerman, B. (2008). *Followership: How followers are creating change and changing leaders.* Boston, MA: Harvard Business Press.

Kilduff, M., & Tsai, W. (2003). *Social networks and organizations.* Thousand Oaks, CA: Sage.

Kirman, A. (2001). Market organization and individual behavior: Evidence from fish markets. In J. E. Rauch & A. Casella (Eds.), *Networks and markets* (pp. 155–195). New York: Russel Sage.

Knoke, D., & Kuklinski, J. H. (1982). *Network analysis.* Beverly Hills, CA: Sage.

Koch, S., & Deetz, S. (1981). Metaphor analysis of social reality in organizations. *Journal of Applied Communication Research, 9*(1), 1–15.

Kogut, B. (2000). The network as knowledge: Generative rules and the emergence of structure. *Strategic Management Journal, 21,* 405–425.

Kohane, I. S., Masys, D. R., & Altman, R. B. (2006). The incidentalome: A threat to genomic medicine. *Journal of the American Medical Association, 296*(2), 212–215.

Kolb, J. A. (1996). Let's bring structure back: A commentary. *Management Communication Quarterly, 9,* 452–465.

Kovecses, Z. (2002). *Metaphor: A practical introduction (p. 7).* New York: Oxford University Press.

Krackhardt, D. (1989). *Graph theoretical dimensions of informal organizations.* Paper presented at the National Meetings of the Academy of Management, Washington, D.C.

Krackhardt, D. (1994). Constraints on the interactive organization as an ideal type. In C. Heckscher & A. Donnelon (Eds.), *The post-bureaucratic organization: New perspectives on organizational change* (pp. 211–222). Thousand Oaks, CA: Sage.

Kratzer, J., Leenders, R. T. A. J., & van Engelen, J. M. L. (2004). Stimulating the potential: Creative performance and communication in innovation teams. *Creativity and Innovation Management, 13,* 63–71.

Krippendorf, K. (1993). Major metaphors of communication and some constructivist reflections on their use. *Cybernetics and Human Knowing, 2*(1), 3–25.

Kuhn, T., & Corman, S. R. (2003). The emergence of homogeneity and heterogeneity in knowledge structures during a planned organizational change. *Communication Monographs, 70,* 198–229.

Lane, P. J., Koka, B. R., & Pathak, S. (2006). The reification of absorptive capacity: A critical review and rejuvenation of the construct. *Academy of Management Review, 31,* 833–863.

Larwood, L. (1992). Don't struggle to scope those metaphors yet. *Group and Organization Management, 17,* 249–254.

Lawrence, P. R., & Lorsch, J. W. (1967). *Organization and environment: Managing differentiation and integration.* Boston, MA: Harvard Business School.

Leavitt, H. J. (1951). Some effects of certain communication patterns on group performance. *Journal of Abnormal and Social Psychology, 46,* 38–50.

Lee, G. K. (2007). The significance of network resources in the race to enter emerging product markets: the convergence of telephony communications and computer networking, 1989–2001. *Strategic Management Journal, 28,* 17–37.

Leifer, R., & Delbecq, A. (1978). Organizational/environmental interchange: A model of boundary spanning activity. *Academy of Management Review, 20*, 40–50.

Lengel, R. H., & Daft, R. L. (1988). The selection of communication media as an executive skill. *Academy of Management Executive, 2*, 225–232.

Leonard-Barton, D., & Deschamps, I. (1988). Managerial influence in the implementation of new technology. *Management Science, 34*, 1252–1265.

Leonard, D. A. (2006). Innovation as a knowledge generation and transfer process. In A. Singhal & J. W. Dearing (Eds.), *Communication of innovations: A journey with Ev Rogers* (pp. 83–111). Thousand Oaks, CA: Sage.

Lichtenstein, E., & Glasgow, R. E. (1992). Smoking cessation: What have we learned over the past decade? *Journal of Counseling and Clinical Psychology, 60*(4), 518–527.

Lichter, I. (1987). *Communication in cancer care.* New York: Churchill Livingstone.

Likert, R. (1967). *The human organization: Its management and value.* Hightstown, NJ: McGraw-Hill.

Lincoln, J. R., & McBride, K. (1985). Resources, homophily, and dependence: Organizational attributes and asymmetric ties in human resource networks. *Social Science Research, 14*, 1–30.

Littlejohn, S. W. (1989). *Theories of human communication* (3rd ed.). Belmont, CA: Wadsworth Publishing Company.

Littlejohn, S. W., & Foss, K. A. (2011). *Theories of human communication* (10th ed.). Long Grove, IL: Waveland Press.

Lorenz, E. H. (1991). Neither friends nor strangers: Informal networks of subcontracting in French industry. In G. Thompson, J. Frances, R. Levacic, & J. Mitchell (Eds.), *Markets, hierarchies and networks: The coordination of social life* (pp. 183–192). Newbury Park, CA: Sage.

Mangham, I. L. (1996). Some consequences of taking Gareth Morgan seriously. In D. Grant & C. Oswick (Eds.), *Metaphor and organizations* (pp. 21–36). Thousand Oaks, CA: Sage.

March, J. G. (1991). Exploration and exploitation in organizational learning. *Organizational Science, 2*, 71–87.

March, J. G. (1994). *A primer on decision making: How decisions happen.* New York: Free Press.

March, J. G., & Simon, H. A. (1958). *Organizations.* New York: John Wiley.

Markey, K. (2007). Twenty-five years of end-user searching, Part 2: Future research directions. *Journal of the American Society for Information Science and Technology, 58*, 1123–1130.

Markus, M. L. (1994). Electronic mail as the medium of managerial choice. *Organization Science, 5*, 502–527.

Marshak, R. J. (1996). Metaphors, metaphoric fields and organizational change. In D. Grant & C. Oswick (Eds.), *Metaphor and organizations* (pp. 147–165). Thousand Oaks, CA: Sage.

Marwell, G., & Schmitt, D. R. (1967). Dimensions of compliance gaining behavior: An empirical analysis. *Sociometry, 30*, 350–364.

McGrath, C., & Krackhardt, D. (2003). Network conditions for organizational change. *Journal of Applied Behavioral Science, 39*, 324–336.

McGuinness, T. (1991). Markets and managerial hierarchies. In G. Thompson, J. F. R. Levacic, & J. Mitchell (Eds.), *Markets, hierarchies, and networks: The coordination of social life* (pp. 66–81). Newbury Park, CA: Sage.

McGuire, W. J. (1989). Theoretical foundations of campaigns. In R. E. Rice & C. K. Atkin (Eds.), *Public communication campaigns* (pp. 43–66). Newbury Park, CA: Sage.

McPhee, R. D. (1988). Vertical communication chains: Toward an integrated approach. *Management Communication Quarterly, 1*, 455–493.

McPherson, M., Smith-Lovin, L., & Brashears, M. E. (2006). Social isolation in America: Changes in core discussion networks over two decades. *American Sociological Review, 71*, 353–375.

Menard, S. (1991). *Longitudinal research*. Thousand Oaks, CA: Sage.

Meyer, A. D. (1984). Mingling decision making metaphors. *Academy of Management Review, 9*, 6–17.

Milardo, R. M. (1983). Social networks and pair relationships: A review of substantive and measurement issues. *Sociology and Social Research, 68*, 1–18.

Miller, V. D., & Jablin, F. M. (1991). Information seeking during organizational entry: Influences, tactics, and a model of the process. *Academy of Management Review, 16*, 92–120.

Minor, M. J. (1983). New directions in multiplexity analysis. In R. S. Burt & M. J. Minor (Eds.), *Applied network analysis: A methodological introduction* (pp. 223–244). Beverly Hills, CA: Sage.

Mohrman, S. A., Tenkasi, R. V., & Mohrman, A. M., Jr. (2003). The role of networks in fundamental organizational change: A grounded analysis. *Journal of Applied Behavioral Science, 39*, 301–323.

Monge, P. R., & Contractor, N. S. (2003). *Theories of communication networks*. New York: Oxford University Press.

Monge, P. R., Edwards, J. A., & Kirste, K. K. (1978). The determinants of communication and communication structure in large organizations: A review of research. In B. D. Rubin (Ed.), *Communication Yearbook 2* (pp. 311–331). New Brunswick, NJ: Transaction Books.

Monge, P. R., & Miller, K. I. (1988). Participative processes in organizations. In G. M. Goldhaber & G. A. Barnett (Eds.), *Handbook of organizational communication* (pp. 213–229). Norwood, NJ: Ablex.

Morgan, G. (1986). *Images of organization*. Beverly Hills, CA: Sage.

Morgan, S. E., King, A. J., & Ivic, R. K. (2011). Using new technologies to enhance health communication research methodology. In T. L. Thompson & R. Parrott (Eds.), *The Routledge handbook of health communication* (2nd ed., pp. 578–592). New York: Routledge.

Morley, D. (1993). Active audience theory: Pendulums and pitfalls *Journal of Communication, 43*, 13–19.

Mukherjee, S. (2010). *The emperor of all maladies: A biography of cancer*. New York: Scribner.

Noar, S. M. (2006). A 10-year retrospective of research in health mass media campaigns: Where do we go from here? *Journal of Health Communication, 11*, 21–42.

Noar, S. M., Palmgreen, P., & Zimmerman, R. S. (2009). Reflections on evaluating health communication campaigns. *Communication Methods and Measures, 3*(1), 105–114.

O'Reilly, C. A., III, & Pondy, L. R. (1979). Organizational communication. In S. Kerr (Ed.), *Organizational behavior* (pp. 119–150). Columbus, OH: Grid.

Oswick, C., Fleming, P., & Hanlon, G. (2011). From borrowing to blending: Rethinking the process of organizational theory building. *Academy of Management Review, 36*(2), 316–337.

Oswick, C., & Grant, D. (1996). The organization of metaphors and the metaphors of organization: where are we and where do we go from here? In D. Grant & C. Oswick (Eds.), *Metaphor and organizations* (pp. 213–226). Thousand Oaks, CA: Sage.

Oswick, C., & Jones, P. (2006). Beyond correspondence? Metaphor in organization theory. *Academy of Management Review, 31*, 483–485.

Owen-Smith, J., & Powell, W. W. (2004). Knowledge networks as channels and conduits: The effects of spillovers in the Boston biotechnology community. *Organization Science, 15*(1), 5–21.

Oxford English Dictionary. (1989). *Oxford English Dictionary*. New York: Oxford University Press.

Pacanowsky, M. E., & O'Donnell Trujillo, N. (1982). Communication and organizational cultures. *Western Journal of Speech Communication, 46*, 115–130.

Paisley, W. (1980). Information and work. In B. Dervin & M. J. Voight (Eds.), *Progress in communication sciences* (Vol. II, pp. 114–165). Norwood, NJ: Ablex.

Paisley, W. (1993). Knowledge utilization: The role of new communication technologies. *Journal of the American Society for Information Science, 44*, 222–234.

Palmer, I., & Dunford, R. (1996). Conflicting use of metaphors: Reconceptualizing their use in the field of organizational change. *Academy of Management Review, 21*, 691–717.

Palmgreen, P., Donohew, L., Lorch, E. P., Hoyle, R. H., & Stephenson, M. T. (2002). Television campaigns and sensation seeking targeting adolescent marijuana use: A controlled time series approach. In R. C. Hornik (Ed.), *Public health communication: Evidence for behavior change* (pp. 35–56). Mahwah, NJ: Lawrence Earlbaum Associates.

Parks, M. R. (1982). Ideology in interpersonal communication: Off the couch and into the world. In M. Burgoon (Ed.), *Communication Yearbook 5* (pp. 79–107). New Brunswick, NJ: Transaction books.

Parks, M. R., & Adelman, M. B. (1983). Communication networks and the development of romantic relationships: An expansion of uncertainty reduction theory. *Human Communication Research, 10*, 55–79.

Parks, M. R., Stan, C. M., & Eggert, L. L. (1983). Romantic involvement and social network involvement. *Social Psychology Quarterly, 46*, 116–131.

Pelz, D. C. (1952). Influence: A key to effective leadership in the first-line supervisor. *Personnel, 29*, 209–217.

Perry-Smith, J. E., & Shalley, C. E. (2003). The social side of creativity: A static and dynamic social network perspective. *Academy of Management Review, 28*, 89–106.

Petrie, H. G. (1979). Metaphor and learning. In A. Ortony (Ed.), *Metaphor and thought* (pp. 439–461). Cambridge: Cambridge University Press.

Petronio, S. (2002). *Boundaries of privacy: Dialectics of disclosure.* Albany, NY: State University of New York Press.

Petronio, S., & Reierson, J. (2009). Regulating the privacy of confidentiality: Grasping the complexities through communication privacy management theory. In T. D. Afifi & W. A. Afifi (Eds.), *Uncertainty, information might management, and disclosure decisions: theories and applications* (pp. 365–383). New York: Routledge.

Pfeffer, J. (1978). *Organizational design.* Arlington Heights, IL: AHM Publishing.

Pfeffer, J. (1982). *Organizations and organization theory.* Boston, MA: Pitman.

Picot, A., Klingenberg, H., & Kranzle, H. P. (1982). Office technology: A report on attitudes and channels selection from field studies in Germany. In M. Burgoon (Ed.), *Communication Yearbook 6.* Beverly Hills, CA: Sage.

Pirolli, P., & Card, S. (1999). Information foraging. *Psychological Review, 106*, 643–675.

Poole, M. S., & McPhee, R. D. (1983). A structurational analysis of organizational climate. In L. L. Putnam & M. E. Pacanowsky (Eds.), *Communication and organizations: An interpretive approach* (pp. 195–220). Beverly Hills, CA: Sage.

Powell, W. W. (1990). Neither market nor hierarchy: Network forms of organization. In S. B. Bacharach (Ed.), *Research in organizational behavior* (pp. 295–336). Norwich, CT: JAI Press.

Provan, K. G., & Milward, H. B. (2001). Do networks really work? A framework for evaluating public-sector organizations. *Public Administration Review, 61,* 414–423.

Putnam, L. L. (1998). Metaphors of communication and organization. In J. S. Trent (Ed.), *Communication: views from the helm for the 21st century* (pp. 145–161). Boston: Allyn and Bacon.

Putnam, L. L. (1999). Shifting metaphors of organizational communication: The rise of discourse perspectives. In P. Salem (Ed.), *Organizational communication and change* (pp. 45–65). Cresskill, NJ: Hampton Press.

Putnam, L. L., & Boys, S. (2006). Revisiting metaphors of organizational communication. Clegg, S. R., Hardy, C., Lawrence, T. B., Nord, W. (Eds.) In *Sage handbook of organization studies* (pp. 541–576). Thousand Oaks, CA: Sage.

Putnam, R. D. (2000). *Bowling alone: The collapse and revival of American community.* New York: Simon & Schuster.

Randolph, W. A., & Finch, F. E. (1977). The relationship between organization technology and the direction and frequency dimensions of task communications. *Human Relations, 30,* 1131–1145.

Reagans, R., & McEvily, B. (2003). Network structure and knowledge transfer: The effect of cohesion and range. *Administrative Science Quarterly, 48,* 240–267.

Real, K. (2008). Information seeking and workplace safety: A field application of the risk perception attitude framework. *Journal of Applied Communication Research, 36,* 339–359.

Reddy, M. J. (1979). The conduit metaphor—a case of frame conflict in our language about language. In A. Ortony (Ed.), *Metaphor and thought* (pp. 284–324). Cambridge: Cambridge University Press.

Rice, R. E. (1993). Media appropriateness: using social presence theory to compare traditional and new organizational media. *Human Communication Research, 19,* 451–484.

Rice, R. E., & Associates (1984). *The new media: Communication, research, and technology.* Beverly Hills, CA: Sage.

Rice, R. E., Grant, A., Schmitz, J., & Torobin, J. (1988). *Organizational information processing, critical mass and social influence: A network approach to predicting the adoption and outcomes of electronic messaging.* Paper presented at the Annual meeting of the International Communication Association, New Orleans, LA.

Rice, R. E., & Shook, D. E. (1990). Relationships of job categories and organizational levels to use of communication channels, including electronic model: A meta-analysis and extension. *Journal of Management Studies, 27,* 196–229.

Richards, W. D. (1985). Data, models, and assumptions in network analysis. In R. D. McPhee & P. K. Tompkins (Eds.), *Organizational communication: Traditional themes and new directions* (pp. 109–128). Beverly Hills, CA: Sage.

Rimal, R. N., Flora, J. A., & Schooler, C. (1999). Achieving improvements in overall health orientation: Effects of campaign exposure, information seeking, and health media use. *Communication Research, 26*(3), 322–348.

Ritti, R. R. (1986). The social bases of organizational knowledge. In L. Thayer (Ed.), *Organization–Communication* (pp. 102–132). Norwood, NJ: Ablex.

Robertson, T. S., & Wortzel, L. H. (1977). Consumer behavior and health care change: The role of mass media. *Consumer Research, 4,* 525–527.

Robinson, M. A. (2010). An empirical analysis of engineers' information behavior. *Journal of the American Society for Information Science and Technology, 61*(4), 640–658.

Rogers, D. P. (1987). The development of the measure of perceived communication openness. *Journal of Business Communication, 24,* 53–61.

Rogers, E. M. (1962). *Diffusion of innovation* (1st ed.). New York: Free Press.

Rogers, E. M. (1995). *Diffusion of innovations* (4th ed.). New York: Free Press.

Rogers, E. M. (2003). *Diffusion of innovations* (5th ed.). New York: Free Press.

Rogers, E. M., & Adhikayra, R. (1979). Diffusion of innovations: An up-to-date review and commentary. In D. Nimmo (Ed.), *Communication Yearbook 3* (pp. 67–81). New Brunswick, NJ: Transaction Books.

Rogers, E. M., & Kincaid, D. L. (1981). *Communication networks: Toward a new paradigm for research.* New York: Free Press.

Rogers, E. M., & Shoemaker, F. F. (1971). *Communication of innovations* (2nd ed.). New York: Free Press.

Rogers, E. M., & Storey, J. D. (1987). Communication campaigns. In C. R. Berger & S. H. Chaffee (Eds.), *Handbook of communication science* (pp. 817–846). Newbury Park, CA: Sage.

Rowley, J. E., & Turner, C. M. D. (1978). *The dissemination of information.* Boulder, CO: Westview Press.

Rowley, T., Behrens, D., & Krackhardt, D. (2000). Redundant governance structures: An analysis of structural and relational embeddedness in the steel and semiconductor industries. *Strategic Management Journal, 21,* 369–386.

Ruchinskas, J. E. (1983). *Predictors of media utility: Influence on managers perception of business communication systems.* Paper presented at the International communication Association, Dallas, TX.

Russo, T. C., & Koesten, J. (2005). Prestige, centrality, and learning: A social network analysis of an online class. *Communication Education, 54,* 254–261.

Salmon, C. T., & Atkin, C. (2003). Using media campaigns for health promotion. In T. L. Thompson, A. M. Dorsey, K. I. Miller, & R. Parrott (Eds.), *Handbook of health communication* (pp. 449–472). Mahwah, NJ: Lawrence Erlbaum Associates.

Schon, D. A. (1979). Generative metaphor: A perspective on problem-setting in social policy. In A. Ortony (Ed.), *Metaphor and thought* (pp. 254–283). Cambridge: Cambridge University Press.

Schramm, W. (1954). *The process and effects of mass communication.* Urbana, IL: University of Illinois Press.

Schramm, W. S. (1972). The nature of communication between humans. In W. Schramm & D. F. Roberts (Eds.), *The process and effects of mass communication* (pp. 3–53). Urbana, IL: University of Illinois Press.

Schramm, W. S. (1973). *Men, messages, and media.* New York: Harper & Row.

Scott, J. (1991). *Social network analysis: A handbook.* Newbury Park, CA: Sage.

Shaw, M. E. (1971). *Group dynamics: The psychology of small group behavior.* New York: McGraw-Hill.

Sherif, M., & Sherif, C. W. (1964). *Reference groups: Exploration into conformity and deviation of adolescents.* Chicago, IL: Henry Regnery.

Short, J., Williams, E., & Christie, B. (1976). *The social psychology of telecommunications.* New York: John Wiley.

Siegel, M., & Biener, L. (2002). The impact of anti-smoking media campaigns and progression to established smoking: results of a longitudinal youth study in Massachusetts. In R. C. Hornik (Ed.), *Public health communication: Evidence for behavior change* (pp. 115–130). Mahwah, NJ: Lawrence Erlbaum Associates.

Simon, H. A. (1987). Making management decisions: The role of intuition and emotion. *Academy of Management Executive, 1,* 57–64.

Simon, H. A. (1991). *Models of my life.* New York: Basic Books.

Simpson, R. L. (1952). Vertical and horizontal communication in formal organizations. *Administrative Science Quarterly, 2,* 188–196.

Sitkin, S. B., Sutcliffe, K. M., & Barrios-Choplin, J. R. (1992). A dual-capacity model of communication media choice in organizations. *Human Communication Research, 18,* 563–598.

Slater, M. D. (2004). Operationalizing and analyzing exposure: The foundation of media effects research. *Journalism and Mass Communication Quarterly, 81,* 168–183.

Smircich, L., & Calas, M. B. (1987). Organizational culture: A critical assessment. In F. M. Jablin, L. L. Putnam, K. H. Roberts, & L. W. Porter (Eds.), *Handbook of organizational communication: An interdisciplinary perspective* (pp. 228–263). Newbury Park, CA: Sage.

Snyder, L. B., & Hamilton, M. A. (2002). A meta-analysis of US of health campaign effects on behavior: Emphasize enforcement, exposure, and new information and beware the secular trend. In R. C. Hornik (Ed.), *Public health communication: Evidence for behavior change.* Mawah, NJ: Lawrence Erlbaum Associates.

Stafford, L. (2003). Maintaining romantic relationships: A summary and analysis of one research program. In D. J. Canary & M. Dainton (Eds.), *Maintaining relationships through communication: Relational, contextual, and cultural variations* (pp. 51–78). Mahwah, NJ: Lawrence Erlbaum Associates.

Stafford, L. (2005). *Maintaining long-distance and cross-residential relationships.* Mahwah, NJ: Lawrence Erlbaum.

Stafford, L., & Canary, D. J. (1991). Maintenance strategies and romantic relationship type, gender and relational characteristics. *Journal of Social and Personal Relationships, 8,* 217–242.

Steinfeld, C. W., Jin, B., & Ku, L. L. (1987). *A preliminary test of a social information processing model of media use in organizations.* Paper presented at the International Communication Association annual conference, Montréal, Canada.

Stohl, C., & Redding, W. C. (1987). Messages and message exchange processes. In F. M. Jablin, L. L. Putnam, K. H. Roberts, & L. W. Porter (Eds.), *Handbook of organizational communication: An interdisciplinary perspective* (pp. 451–502). Newbury Park, CA: Sage.

Sullivan, C. B. (1995). Preferences for electronic mail in organizational communication tasks. *Journal of Business Communication, 32,* 49–65.

Surowiecki, J. (2004). *The wisdom of crowds: Why the many are smarter than the few and how collective wisdom shapes business, economies, societies, and nations.* New York: Random House.

Swedberg, R. (1994). Markets as social structures. In N. J. Smelser & R. Swedberg (Eds.), *The handbook of economic sociology* (pp. 255–282). Princeton, NJ: Princeton University Press.

Szulanski, G. (1996). Exploring internal stickiness: Impediments to the transfer of best practice within the firm. *Strategic Management Journal, 17,* 27–43.

Szulanski, G. (2003). *Sticky knowledge: Barriers to knowing in the firm.* Thousand Oaks, CA: Sage.

Tannenbaum, A. S. (1966). *Social psychology of the work organization.* London: Tavistock.

Taylor, A., & Greve, H. R. (2006). Superman or the Fantastic Four? Knowledge combination and experience in innovative teams. *Academy of Management Journal, 49,* 723–740.

Thomas, J. B., Clark, S. M., & Gioia, D. A. (1993). Strategic sensemaking and organizational performance: Linkages among scanning, interpretation, action, and outcomes. *Academy of Management Journal, 36,* 239–270.

Tsoukas, T. (1991). The missing link: A transformational view of metaphors in organizational science. *Academy of Management Review, 16*(3), 566–585.

Tushman, M. L. (1978). Technical communication in R&D laboratories: The impact of project work characteristics. *Academy of Management Journal, 21,* 624–645.

Tushman, M. L. (1979). Work characteristics and subunit communication structure: A contingency analysis. *Administrative Science Quarterly, 24,* 82–98.

Tushman, M. L., & Scanlan, T. J. (1981a). Boundary spanning individuals: Their role in information transfer and their antecedents. *Academy of Management Journal, 24,* 289–305.

Tushman, M. L., & Scanlan, T. J. (1981b). Characteristics and external orientations of boundary spanning individuals. *Academy of Management Journal, 24,* 83–98.

Uzzi, B., & Spiro, J. (2005). Collaboration and creativity: The small world problem. *American Journal of Sociology, 111,* 447–504.

Valente, T. (2006). Communication network analysis and the diffusion of innovations. In A. Singhal & J. W. Dearing (Eds.), *A journey with Ev Rogers* (pp. 61–82). Thousand Oaks, CA: Sage.

Valente, T. W. (1995). *Network models of the diffusion of innovations.* Cresskill, NJ: Hampton Press.

Van de Ven, A. H. (1976). On the nature, formation, and maintenance of relations among organizations. *Academy of Management Review, 1,* 24–36.

Van de Ven, A. H. (1986). Central problems in the management of innovation. *Management Science, 32,* 590–607.

Van de Ven, A. H., Delbecq, A. L., & Koenig, R. (1976). Determinants of coordination modes within organizations. *Administrative Science Quarterly, 41,* 322–338.

Van den Bulte, C., & Lillien, G. L. (2001). Medical innovation revisited: Social contagion versus marketing effort. *American Journal of Sociology, 106,* 1409–1435.

Von Hayek, F. (1991). Spontaneous ('grown') order and organized ('made') order. In G. Thompson, J. Frances, R. Levacic, & J. Mitchell (Eds.), *Markets, hierarchies, and networks: The coordination of social life* (pp. 293–301). Newbury Park, CA: Sage.

Walther, J. B. (1994). Anticipated ongoing interaction versus channel effects on relational communication and computer-mediated interaction. *Human Communication Research, 20,* 473–501.

Watts, D. J. (2002). A simple model of global cascades on random networks. *Proceedings of the National Academy of Sciences of the United States of America, 99,* 5766–5771.

Watts, D. J. (2003). *Six degrees: The science of the connected age.* New York: W. W. Norton.

Weedman, J. (1992). Informal and formal channels in boundary-spanning communication. *Journal of American Society for Information Science, 43,* 257–267.

Weick, K. E. (1969). *The social psychology of organizing.* Reading, MA: Addison-Wesley.

Weick, K. E. (1976). Educational organizations as loosely coupled systems. *Administrative Science Quarterly, 21*, 1–19.

Weimann, G. (1983). The strength of weak conversational ties in the flow of information and influence. *Social Networks, 5*, 245–267.

Woelful, J., Cody, M. J., Gillham, J., & Holmes, R. A. (1980). Basic premises of multidimensional attitude change theory: An experimental analysis. *Academy of Management Journal, 6*, 153–167.

Woodward, J. (1965). *Industrial organization.* London: Oxford University Press.

Wright, K. B. (1999). Computer-mediated support groups: An examination of relationships among social support, perceived stress, and coping strategies. *Communication Quarterly, 47*(4), 402–414.

Zahra, S. A., & George, G. (2002). Absorptive capacity: A review, reconceptualization, and extension. *Academy of Management Review, 27*, 185–203.

Zaltman, G. (1994). Knowledge disavowal in organizations. In R. H. Kilmann, K. W. Thomas, D. P. Slevin, R. Nath, & S. L. Jerrell (Eds.), *Producing useful knowledge in organizations* (pp. 173–187). San Francisco, CA: Jossey-Bass.

Zimbardo, P. G. (1960). Involvement and communication discrepancy as determinants of opinion conformity. *Journal of Abnormal and Social Psychology, 60*, 86–94.

Zimmerman, S., Sypher, B. D., & Haas, J. W. (1996). A communication metamyth in the workplace: The assumption that more is better. *Journal of Business Communication, 33*, 185–204.

Zipf, G. (1949). *Human behavior and the principle of least effort: An introduction to human ecology.* New York: Addison-Wesley.

Index

OTHER TITLES IN OUR CORPORATE COMMUNICATION COLLECTION

Debbie D. DuFrene, Stephen F. Austin State University, Collection Editor

- *Managing Investor Relations: Strategies for Effective Communication* by Alexander Laskin
- *Fundamentals of Writing for Marketing and Public Relations: A Step-by-Step Guide for Quick and Effective Results* by Janet Mizrahi
- *Communication Strategies for Today's Managerial Leader* by Deborah Britt Roebuck
- *Communication Strategies for Virtual Teams* by Debbie D. DuFrene and Carol M. Lehman
- *Corporate Communication: Tactical Guidelines for Strategic Practice* by Michael B. Goodman and Peter B. Hirsch
- *Communicating Business Responsibility: Strategies, Concepts and Cases for Integrated Marketing Communication* by Roger N. Conaway and Oliver Laasch

---

Announcing the Business Expert Press Digital Library

Concise E-books Business Students Need for Classroom and Research

This book can also be purchased in an e-book collection by your library as

- a one-time purchase,
- that is owned forever,
- allows for simultaneous readers,
- has no restrictions on printing, and
- can be downloaded as PDFs from within the library community.

Our digital library collections are a great solution to beat the rising cost of textbooks. e-books can be loaded into their course management systems or onto student's e-book readers.

The **Business Expert Press** digital libraries are very affordable, with no obligation to buy in future years. For more information, please visit **www.businessexpertpress.com/librarians**. To set up a trial in the United States, please contact **Adam Chesler** at *adam.chesler@businessexpertpress .com* for all other regions, contact **Nicole Lee** at *nicole.lee@igroupnet.com*.